The Manly Art of
Raising a Daughter

ALAN MIGLIORATO

THE
MANLY
ART
OF RAISING A
DAUGHTER

SOPHIA INSTITUTE PRESS
MANCHESTER, NEW HAMPSHIRE

Sophia Institute Press
Box 5284, Manchester, NH 03108
1-800-888-9344

www.SophiaInstitute.com

Sophia Institute Press® is a registered trademark of Sophia Institute.

Library of Congress Cataloging-in-Publication Data

Names: Migliorato, Alan, author.
Title: The manly art of raising a daughter / Alan Migliorato.
Description: Manchester, New Hampshire : Sophia Institute Press, 2018.
Identifiers: LCCN 2018041359 | ISBN 9781622826643 (pbk. : alk. paper)
Subjects: LCSH: Fathers and daughters—Religious aspects—Christianity. |
   Child rearing—Religious aspects—Christianity. | Parenting—Religious
   aspects—Christianity.
Classification: LCC BV4529.17 .M54 2018 | DDC 248.8/421—dc23 LC record
available at https://lccn.loc.gov/2018041359

First printing

To my wife and three daughters:
Thank you for teaching me how to be manly.

CONTENTS

PREFACE

The idea for this book came from my experiences in raising three beautiful daughters. I have learned more about being a man from them and from my wife than I would ever have imagined. I have included in these pages some of my successes and some of my mistakes and have described my transition from *thinking* I was a man to *becoming* a man.

God is amazing. If I lived for a thousand years, I would never be deserving of the blessings He has bestowed upon me. Every day, I am grateful that He sees more in me than I see in myself and has given me this incredible opportunity to raise a family.

My family has helped me to grow closer to God and to put others before myself, and has shown me what being manly really means.

The Manly Art of Raising a Daughter

Introduction

It's never too late to learn the manly art of raising a daughter. No matter what stage of fatherhood you're in, there's no time like the present to start being the type of real man your daughter can be proud of.

This book is probably going to ruffle a few feathers. Nevertheless, the truth needs to be written. Men have forgotten not only how to be men but also what it takes to be a man. Chivalrous behavior has been twisted and misconstrued as chauvinism over the years and is now thought of as something offensive. Opening the door for a lady has come to be seen as a man telling a woman she is weak, instead of being seen as a polite gesture. It seems as if men are afraid to act like men because they worry they will offend someone.

Has the formula been lost for fatherhood as well? Men have stopped being involved in the lives of their daughters and have allowed the family unit to weaken. The word "father" has been replaced with "baby daddy," and women are being forced to raise families on their own. Men are not persevering in their duties as fathers.

So, what happened to manly men? Did society change its idea of how men are expected to behave, or have men just become weaker over time? Regardless of why, the fact remains: men need to step it up when it comes to raising their children.

As you read this book, you will find things that go against the grain of "normal" social teaching. That's okay! Discomfort encourages the most growth. Just keep an open mind, and let the wisdom sink in!

Okay, ready for the first taboo topic? Here it is: men are supposed to be the heads of their households. Wow! Does this mean that men are supposed to lead their families, and women are supposed to let them? In a way, yes! Here's where I lose most female readers.

"What? Wait a second here!" you might object. "I thought this book was about men raising their daughters." It is! But in order for men to raise their daughters correctly, they need to have a clear understanding of their role as the heads of their households and not be ashamed to take charge of their families.

You may disagree with the statement that a man is the head of his household. Your wife may even be a big part of the reason you disagree! Nonetheless, it's true and extremely important to your success as a father and a husband to put trust in this statement.

Although the roles God gives men are very different from the roles He gives women, those roles are equally important. God sees men and women as spiritual equals, and it is our job as men raising daughters to make sure we let them know they are equal to men.

It's true that, physically speaking, most men are stronger than women. Women are strong in a different way. They are designed to give birth (men don't do that), to breast-feed babies (men don't do that), and to nurture their children (men do this differently than most women). God designed men and women this way for a reason, and we need to be grateful for the way He created us.

If you are still reading this book and are willing to take a chance at becoming a better father to your daughter—and a better husband to your wife—good for you! If you have already put this book down, in which case you have not seen this sentence anyway, you are missing out on a great opportunity!

CHAPTER 1

Introduce Her to God

For the past twenty years I have owned and operated my own business. Anyone who has attempted this venture knows how difficult it can be in the beginning. I worked seven days a week and about twelve to fourteen hours a day on average, trying to build a customer base so I could make a profit. I was young and was eager to impress my family with my hard work.

When I left for work in the morning, my daughter would usually just be waking up, and when I got home at night, she was just about ready to go to bed. I would have her sit with me on the couch and read to her before bedtime until she fell asleep. Then I would carry her to her room and put her to bed. That was all the time I had to spend with her.

On Sundays, my wife would take my daughter to church with my mom and afterward come to see me at work for a few minutes before heading home, or to lunch, or whatever they had planned for the day.

One Sunday, my family came to visit me at work, as usual, and as they were getting ready to leave, I heard my daughter say, "Why doesn't Daddy go to church or to lunch with us?" My heart broke. I never liked working on weekends and always felt as if I were missing out on family time, but I figured that's what I was expected to do in order to give my family what they needed.

The truth is, instead of giving my family what they really needed, I was just giving them money. In reality, I was showing my daughter that money came first. This is a very dangerous message to send to daughters at any age. They need to know that they are the most important things in our lives, above money, above personal desires, above all worldly possessions.

Fathers need to show their daughters that they hold certain relationships to be sacred and above all else. Daughters need to know that their fathers are able to prioritize life values. And they need to know that spending time with God is *required* for their souls to be fulfilled.

If their souls are not fulfilled by God, they are left with an empty feeling. This emptiness is what women end up with when they have a weak or absent father or father figure in their lives. A father does not need to be physically absent for his daughter to feel as though he is not there for her. Some men are absent to their families even though their families see them daily.

Women who are left with this empty feeling from having an absent father usually end up trying to fill that space with other men who will end up disappointing them. Jesus is the only man who will never disappoint your daughter, and she needs to know that.

As fathers, we all make mistakes that disappoint our daughters. Teach your daughter that putting her trust and faith in Jesus will never end in disappointment. Help her to understand the meaning of devotion, and make sure you lead by example.

Okay, back to my story. The morning after hearing my daughter ask why I was missing church and lunch on Sundays, my wife told me about another comment from my daughter. I had left for an early appointment at work before my daughter woke up. When she got up, she looked around the house for me and, not finding me, started crying. My wife asked her what was wrong, and my daughter said, "I don't have a daddy; he's not here anymore." Hearing that story made me sad. It made me think too. I considered how I could change my behaviors and actions so that I could be there for my family in more ways and not just provide them with money to buy things.

Immediately I started making changes. I closed my business on Saturdays and Sundays, and I started waking my daughter up earlier to tell her I loved her and to spend at least a few minutes with her before I left for work. I have kept this tradition to this day: I never leave my house without telling everyone in my family that I love them.

I did not want to lose my business, but, a million times more than that, I did not want to lose my family. I prayed a lot, asking God to help me take care of my family and thanking Him for allowing me to see what was really important in life.

Some amazing things happened when I started closing on weekends. I started making more money than I had ever made before! I felt refreshed because I was not getting burned out from my business, and I was happy about getting to spend time with my family. I enjoyed going places with them and doing things I did not take the opportunity to do before.

The next step for me was to reduce my business hours so I was not working so late during the week. Instead of working from 7:00 a.m. to 9:00 p.m., I started opening at 8:30 and closing at 6:00. Again, I immediately started to feel more refreshed, I had even more time to spend with my family, and I kept seeing a rise in revenue from my efforts.

Even though it was nice to make more money, what amazed me was that I was really enjoying my family time and starting to gain an understanding of what it means to become a real man.

A real man spends time with his family. He spends his time and energy to make sure his family is supported not only financially, but emotionally and spiritually as well. I started to make sure I put my family first in all things.

When my daughter had a field trip or a school party, needed a chaperone, or had a dance recital, or whatever she was doing, I was there for it. When she needed a coach for her sports teams, I stepped up. But on Sundays, I made sure I always set aside time to go to church with my family no matter what else was happening.

Closing on the weekends and having shorter working hours during the week meant taking time away from clients and business. It also meant losing potential income from time to time, as well as a few very demanding clients, which was a good thing ultimately!

I can just imagine that many of you are thinking, "Well, that's easy for the guy writing this book; he owns his own business, so it's easier for him to take time for his family than it is for me." Not true.

Think about this scenario for a minute: let's assume you are missing out on two hundred dollars because you decided to go to your daughter's basketball game instead of working. Now, imagine that someone walks up to you at the game and tells you that he will give you two hundred dollars to walk away from the game and not watch it—and to ignore your daughter during the game. Would you take the money, or would you tell this guy to take a hike?

No matter how much money is offered, my daughter is more important to me, just as your daughter should be more important to you. Get your priorities in order before it is too late. As your daughter grows, she will not remember how much money you earn, but she will remember the time you spend together.

INTRODUCE HER TO GOD

Time cannot be purchased; it is the most precious commodity we have. Everything a father does sends a message to his daughter. She is taking mental notes and learning behaviors that will later be expressed through her actions. If you are not there for her now, she will replace you with a man who will be there for her—and, more than likely, will use her for his own gratification. She will always pass up Mr. Right for Mr. Right Now!

The value of attending church together as a family became apparent to me as my daughters grew. The structure, worship, and respect that going to church together creates for a family are priceless. Knowing that God is greater than anything we will face in our lives is very calming.

God's love for us as His children is the perfect example of how we fathers are supposed to lead our families. If God is our Father and we are to follow His rules and laws, then our daughters will understand the same structure when it comes to the rules we, as fathers, set for our families to follow. If the rules we set for our daughters are based on God's rules, it should be an easy transition for daughters to follow their fathers' rules.

But what does that look like in reality? How can we set guidelines for our children when God gives us free will to follow, or not to follow, His rules? He asks us to respect our fathers and mothers. If we are following God's rules, then any other rule we put in place will be followed. Our children do not have to follow the rule happily; they just have to follow it. Set guidelines and rules for your daughter, and stick to them. Be reasonable, be understanding, be loving, and stick to what you say.

Bringing your daughter to understand that she is created in God's image, and that God is great, will help as she grows and matures. Other people's opinions will not matter nearly as much to her, especially when mean girls at school tell her they don't like her hair, her shoes, her clothes, her nose, her eyes, or whatever. Knowing that she has been created in the image of God will free her from trying to make others like her for who they want her to be. Instead she will become her own person and know that God is all that matters.

SUCCESS STORY

My daughters are now fourteen, seventeen, and twenty. Recently my twenty-year-old flew to New York to visit a friend who had moved there. They had a great time visiting and catching up on what was happening in their lives. Her last full day in New York was on a Sunday, and her friend wanted to spend the day shopping and hanging out.

My daughter asked her friend where the closest Catholic church was because she needed to find out the Mass times before she planned anything else. Her friend said she didn't know and suggested that my daughter skip Mass since it was their last day together in New York. My daughter said she needed to go to church but would see if there was an early Mass so they could go shopping and spend the day together afterward. She got on the Internet at her friend's apartment, found a Catholic church close by, and saw that there was a Mass there at 8:00 a.m.

The next morning, she got on the subway to go to Mass but got lost trying to find the church and missed the early Mass. She texted her friend to let her know that she would attend a 10:00 a.m. Mass at another church. Her friend said she understood, and after Mass they spent the rest of the day together.

When my daughter came home, she told me all about the trip and how she and her friend shopped, ate at some really great restaurants, and so forth. She told me about getting lost trying to get to church and said that she saw many sights she never would have seen otherwise.

I was truly impressed to hear of my daughter's determination to get to church. She hadn't hesitated to tell her friend that she needed to go to church before she could do anything else. She thought nothing of it when she missed the early Mass at the first church and then found another church, instead of giving up and going back to her friend's apartment. She also put aside spending time and having fun shopping on her last day in New York to make sure she fulfilled her obligation to God.

I brought all these things up and told her I was proud of her. She replied that she didn't think anything of putting those things aside because it was not an option for her to miss Mass. Now, that's a girl who has her priorities in order!

The most important thing a man can do for his family is to make sure they go to church together—every Sunday. Yes, even if you are on vacation. Yes, even if it's raining. Yes, even if you really want to watch a football game on TV. No matter what else is going on, demand that your family go to church together.

This sets up a duty-based philosophy for your family and lets them know that spending time with God, their Father in Heaven, is important and takes precedence over all else.

I constantly see fathers fail to lead their families by example. I am one of the youth group leaders at my parish. There are girls I mentor whose fathers I have never seen at church. These girls constantly tell me how they struggle in their relationships with their fathers. I encourage them not to give up on their fathers and to keep reaching out. But that can work only when their fathers are there to reach back to them.

THE MANLY ART OF RAISING A DAUGHTER

Daughters should not have to be the only ones reaching; a man should reach out to his daughter instead of waiting for her to reach out to him. He should put aside his pride and focus on being the type of leader God calls all men to be in their families.

Eventually, fathers who are absent to their daughters will realize that they missed out on a great opportunity to mentor and be an example of the way a man should act. But by then it can be difficult to reverse the damage that has been done. It is not impossible, because nothing is impossible with God, but it can be difficult.

If you feel that damage has been done to your relationship with your daughter, take a step to fix the problem.

Being manly means constantly putting your insecurities aside and humbling yourself to be there for your daughter, no matter what happens. Being manly means that you will never stop loving your daughter, no matter what she does or fails to do.

The result of fulfilling our obligations to God results in our being fulfilled at the same time. God makes sure we are rewarded spiritually for making time for Him. He knows us and wants to see us and hear from us regularly. He also wants to see us raising our families to respect and worship Him, without fail. Raise your daughter to keep God first in all things, and everything else in this book and in her life will fall right into place.

We are designed in God's image, and this should remind us that we are made for greatness. God gives us the perfect example of how we are supposed to lead our families. He is the Good Shepherd who guides with a loving hand, not with an iron fist. He demands respect but allows us free will. He gives us what we need, not necessarily what we think we need. God knows everything about us, more than we will ever understand ourselves. Are you leading your family with the same care and authority?

TAKE ACTION

1. Stop working on Sundays.
2. Teach your daughter that spending time with God comes before everything else.
3. Go to church every Sunday with your family, and sit next to your wife.
4. After church, enjoy your family time together, even if you don't do anything special.
5. Talk with your family about the readings you heard in church.
6. Lead your family as the Good Shepherd leads us—with love, understanding, and a guiding hand. Lead by example, and not by words alone.

CHALLENGE YOURSELF

Your challenge is to take your entire family to church this Sunday. No excuses! Spend time worshipping with your family, and lead them to God. Enforce the "no cell phones" rule for everyone in church. Keep focused on God, and insist that your family do the same. After church, have a meal together, and discuss the readings you just heard. Then spend the rest of the day with your family, enjoying their company. Do not work in any way—no e-mails, texts, phone calls, and so forth. This may seem simple to some of you and impossible to others. If you start creating new habits for your family, they will follow your lead. Begin your path to being manly, and lead your family to God.

Manly men take action—do this challenge now!

CHAPTER 2

Know Her Friends

Any of my daughters will tell you that one of my favorite sayings is: "Eagles fly with eagles, and turkeys flock with turkeys." The meaning of this statement is that you are a reflection of the people you surround yourself with, and vice versa. Teaching your daughter to surround herself with great friends can help her build successful relationships throughout life.

Fathers need to lead by example. Do you surround yourself with solid friendships? Are the men you consider friends the type of men you would want your daughter to be around? Do your friends have integrity, or are they lacking in that department? Be honest!

Whether you like it or not, your daughter is influenced in one way or another by the people she surrounds herself with. Knowing her friends is extremely important. Understanding the type of people your daughter chooses to associate with can give you great insight into how your daughter views herself.

It's human nature to choose friends who have similar interests and tastes. Whether your daughter and her friends like the same type of music, play the same sport, read the same books, or just have a few classes together, there is some common element drawing them together and bonding them to one another.

Knowing your daughter's friends does not mean that you need to become "one of the crowd" when she is sitting with her friends and talking about boys, painting nails, studying for a test, and so forth. Let her have her space! What I am suggesting is that you take note of how her friends act when they walk into your house, the things they say, what their interests are, and their overall demeanor. Did they shake your hand and look you in the eye as they introduced themselves? Or did they walk right past you and completely ignore you?

First impressions are important. Although adolescents are still learning how to navigate through introductions, it is important to pay attention to the way they act around you for the first time.

And as important as the first impression is, the second impression can be just as significant. It can tell you even more than the first impression because your daughter's friends will have let their guard down and will be more likely to be themselves.

If you think you know your daughter well, get to know her friends. Then you will really know her! Her choice in friends can tell a lot about what qualities she considers endearing. Does she choose funny friends who are goofy all the time, or reserved ones who keep quiet until spoken to? Are her friends all honor-roll students, or are they always in detention? Are they athletes or in theatrical productions—or both? All these interests can tell which qualities your daughter finds important.

Getting to know your daughter's friends' parents is also a good way to gauge personalities. When my daughters were younger, there were many times when their friends' parents would drop them off at my house for the first time without even coming in to meet my wife and me. They would just drop their kids off and leave! When you drop your daughter off at someone's house for the first time, get out of the car, put the phone down, and go inside to meet the people who are going to be supervising your daughter!

Then, when you pick your daughter up from someone's house, don't merely text her when you're outside. Go to the door to let her know you are there to pick her up. It may sound ridiculous, but being present and staying involved in every aspect of your daughter's life will help your relationship in countless ways.

For the most part, I have been impressed with the friends my daughters have chosen. There have been times, however, when they made friends who I could clearly see were not good for them. In these situations, I don't suggest coming right out and saying you don't like your daughter's friend, unless you are asked directly to give your opinion.

Why don't I suggest this? Simple: once you say you don't like someone she chose for a friend, she will stop bringing that person around. Sounds like a win-win, right? Not really. Just because your daughter is not bringing that friend to your house, it does not mean she will stop hanging around with that friend. It just means that instead of hanging around with her friend in front of you, she will do it behind your back.

That type of behavior can set your relationship up for failure. It can cause your daughter to think that as long as you are not seeing the bad choices she makes, she has nothing to worry about. The very last type of thinking pattern you want your daughter to have is, "What my dad doesn't know won't hurt him." This type of hide-and-seek behavior can be very damaging.

Your daughter needs to see for herself the reasons you are not fond of this friend—without your coming right out and telling her. That's the tricky part. Asking questions to lead your daughter to self-discovery can be one way of helping her to see that there is a problem.

SUCCESS STORY

My daughter had a friend who I could clearly see was trouble. The attitude with which this girl addressed me, the type of clothes she wore—or hardly wore—the lies she told, the way she spoke about her parents and teachers: everything this girl did screamed, "Run—find a better friend!"

Even making bad choices in friends can reveal something about how your daughter sees herself. The qualities she sees in her friends can be clarified simply by asking, "What makes you choose this person as a friend?" or, "What do you like about this person?" It really clears things up when you find out what your daughter sees in the friends she has chosen to surround herself with.

Maybe it was the rebellious attitude of this girl that had attracted my daughter's friendship. There is a possibility that this was my daughter's way of telling me she wanted to spread her wings a little and gain some independence. It could be that my daughter had not noticed the things I saw in her choice of friend. Whatever the reason, the bad qualities my daughter was overlooking in this friend were far more damaging than any good qualities there were.

When I would talk to this girl around my daughter, I would ask about her home life and about how things were going for her in school. She would usually tell me that she got detention again because the teacher hated her, but she was only talking a little bit, and everyone else was talking, too, at the same time. Or she would say that her parents were upset with her and being unfair with her because they were always angry and took it out on her.

When I would ask specifically what she did to get in trouble with her parents this time, she would say things like, "I only snuck out to walk around the block with my boyfriend at night," or, "They are mad because I am failing English class, but the teacher hates me, and they don't want to listen to me about it." Whatever the reason was, I would just listen and ask more questions. I would often ask this girl questions that were designed to help her be self-reflective, such as, "Do you think you would be in trouble if you waited until the next day to walk around the block with your boyfriend, instead of sneaking out at night?" Usually she would respond by saying that her parents would find something to be upset about, no matter what she did.

My daughter started seeing a pattern in her friend when she heard us talk. I did not bring it up to my daughter; she brought it up to me. She said, "You know, I don't think I am going to hang out with this girl anymore. She is always getting in trouble, and I don't want to be seen as a troublemaker." My daughter said that she felt her friend was always blaming other people for the trouble she got herself into, and it was annoying. Eventually, and with careful guidance, my daughter saw what I saw and stopped hanging around with this girl.

It wasn't that I disliked this girl; I simply thought she was making horrible decisions. Even though I did not like this girl's decision-making, however, she was always welcome at my house. I would rather have her and my daughter at my house so I could keep an eye on them than have my daughter at her house or wherever else they ended up. This is not to say I did not trust my daughter, but she was still learning temptation resistance and the power of peer pressure, and I thought it better for them to be nearby.

This approach may sound very judgmental. It is! We are supposed to judge the actions of others. We are *not* supposed to judge other people; that is God's job. But we are supposed to teach our daughters to judge the actions of the people they are considering having as friends. Although it's very common to hear people say, "You have no right to judge me," we have every right—actually, it is our duty—to judge the actions of those we surround ourselves with. This is an important lesson to teach your daughter.

If you don't think you judge people's actions, you are not being honest with yourself. Want proof? Okay. How many friends do you have who are drug dealers, child molesters, murderers, or bank robbers? Hopefully none! That would be an awful choice to make and an awful example to set for your daughter. Luckily, you have used your power of judgment to keep these types of people away from your family.

Asking your daughter's friends questions and listening to their responses can be a great way to get to know them. It's a great way to know your daughter as well. The first time any of my daughters brings a new friend into our house, I always take a minute or two to see if the friend is hungry, thirsty, or needs anything, and just to talk for a few minutes. I find out where they know each other from and practice active listening—meaning that I ask questions based on the responses the friend gives to my first question.

Asking open-ended questions can help open the door to other questions. For example, "Tell me about how you girls met" can be a better question than "So, you met in math class, right?" It offers an opportunity to hear a response longer than one word.

I want my daughter and her friends to feel at home in my house at all times. My daughters know that their friends are always welcome at my house—and their friends know this too. It is important for them to know that they always have a safe place to go. Setting up a warm, welcoming home for them, where there is food readily available and good conversation, is important to creating a deep bond with your daughter's friends.

Does this mean you need to open a buffet in your house? No, of course not. It also does not mean that you need to feed all the kids in the neighborhood and let them run all over your house. Your daughter and her friends need to be taught to respect you and your things. They need to know you are being gracious. You don't have to make a ton of money to create a welcome and safe place for your daughter and her friends.

I encourage my daughters to have their friends over for sleepovers, pool parties, marshmallow roasts, or whatever else they want to do. I want to know my daughters' friends and understand who they are so I can see how my daughters' other circles of influence work. To think that kids are not influenced by anyone other than their parents is foolish.

Knowing the people your daughter hangs around with allows a few things to happen. First, you get to know your daughter's friends' likes and dislikes. Second, your daughter's friends get to know you. Third, it shows you really care about and are involved in your daughter's life.

Having your daughter's friends get to know you can have many advantages. I have had my daughters' friends ask me for advice on extremely important issues at pivotal points in their lives. That sort of relationship can happen only when you are close to your daughter. Your daughter's friends will see the bond the two of you share and will feel safe in opening up to you as well.

It never fails that when I ask my daughters' friends if they tell their own dads the things they talk to me about, they say no; they are not that close to their dads. It makes me sad to hear that these fathers are not taking the opportunity to get to know their daughters. Don't miss out on having a relationship with your daughter and her friends, which can create a helpful mentoring opportunity.

Girls who do not have a strong bond with their fathers are likely to have many more problems socially, mentally, physically, and spiritually. Daughters without this strong relationship are much more likely to have underage sexual contact, experiment with drinking and drugs, have poor academic achievement, commit crime, and attempt suicide.

Fathers are given a great opportunity to mold and enhance the lives of their daughters. Step up to the challenge! The relationship you have with your daughter will permeate everything she does.

TAKE ACTION

1. Make your home a welcoming place for your daughter to bring her friends to hang out.
2. Talk to your daughter's friends and get to know them.
3. Find out what interests your daughter has in common with her friends.
4. Find out how your daughter is different from her friends.
5. Take notice of how your daughter's friends greet you and behave at your house.
6. Teach your daughter to be aware of damaging behaviors and toxic friendships.
7. Teach your daughter how to judge others' behaviors.

CHALLENGE YOURSELF

Your challenge is to ask your daughter to have a few friends spend the night at your house. Take time to talk with and get to know the people your daughter surrounds herself with. Play a card game, twenty questions, or a board game with your daughter and her friends. After her friends have gone home, ask your daughter to tell you why she likes each of them. Ask her what she has in common with her friends, as well as how she is different from them. Get her thinking, and listen to what she has to say!

Manly men take action—do this challenge now!

CHAPTER 3

Teach Her to Fight

My father was a professional boxer. From the time I was able to walk, I was at the gym with him while he trained. I remember being in boxing gloves at the age of three or four and hitting the punching bag while my father encouraged me and instructed me on the correct form. He taught me how to defend myself and hold my hands up in front of me so I would not get hit. I learned to keep a safe distance from my enemies and to be aware of my surroundings, to interpret my opponent's movements, and to watch for an opening so I could strike.

What a wonderful gift my father had given me at a young age! These lessons on fighting transferred into all other aspects of my life. I learned to keep my distance from my enemies not only physically, but emotionally and spiritually as well. I knew not to get too close to people in my life who were toxic and to keep myself protected from their attacks. Sometimes that meant ignoring what people had to say, and sometimes it meant that I needed to stand my ground and fight for what I felt was worth battling for.

As I grew up, I frequently heard the phrase "Never start a fight, and never run away from one if you have no choice." This was very important to my father and to the way he raised me. He never wanted me to become a bully. He would always say that the skills he taught me were not to be used to push people around. He also warned me that there might be times when I would not be able to talk my way out of a fight, no matter how I tried. He said some people would not listen to reason and that I should never be a coward.

He was training me for my future and giving me confidence, whether intentionally or not. As I grew up, there were times when I did my absolute best to avoid confrontations with others and tried not to look for a problem. But problems sometimes found me, and I was left with no option but to protect myself.

Raising my own daughters, I have implemented the same rule: "Never start a fight, and never run away from one if you have no choice." It is very important that girls know how to fight, and it is just as important that their fathers teach them to fight. Am I condoning violence? Absolutely not. Am I saying that there are times when a girl will need to know she is more than capable of defending herself against anyone who attacks her? Definitely.

But what kind of fighting am I talking about? Do I mean that girls should be capable of punching and kicking to defend themselves? Well, yes, but there's much more to it than that.

It is important for a girl to be taught by her father to protect and defend herself, not only physically, but emotionally and spiritually as well. There may be times, of course, when she has to be physical and defend herself, and she will need the confidence she has learned from her father, a real man who knows she is capable of defending herself. Unfortunately, there are other types of attacks that happen daily that your daughter will need to be prepared to defend herself against at all times.

Some parents feel the need to step in every time a problem arises in their daughters' lives—to fix a problem with grading in school, to fix an argument between their daughter and her best friend, to deal with a boy who has been disrespectful toward her, and so forth. Although the intention of stepping in to fix problems for your daughter may be understandable, this is the worst way to teach your daughter how to fight for herself.

This type of parental behavior only weakens your daughter's belief in herself and makes her think you do not believe in her ability to handle things on her own.

Am I saying that there is never a time to step in and take charge of a situation? Not exactly. What I am saying is that your daughter needs to know that you have the faith and confidence that she can resolve problems on her own.

Be there for your daughter. Let her know that it is okay to feel upset, angry, or sad. Ask her how she plans to handle situations she is faced with. Knowing that her father, a strong, God-centered man in her life, thinks she can handle problems on her own means much more to her than you can imagine.

SUCCESS STORY

When my daughter turned sixteen, she was given a used car as a gift. She was shown how to take care of this vehicle, how to tell whether the tires needed air, how to watch and listen for anything that did not sound normal in the vehicle while driving, and so forth.

My daughter and her friends wanted to spend a day at a local theme park, and she asked me if she could go and if she could drive her friends there in her newly acquired car. I told her that I trusted her and did not have any problem with her driving her friends to the park. After letting me know what time she would be home, she set out to pick up her friends and headed to the park. Around 6:00 p.m., I got a phone call from her telling me that her car would not start. She said the dome light inside the car was left on, and the battery was drained.

My normal response to these situations is to give my girls the opportunity to resolve these issues themselves. So I said, "What are you planning on doing to get it taken care of?" She said, "I already contacted the park security officer by calling from a phone in the parking garage. He is on his way to give the battery a jump to get the car started. I already took care of resolving the problem. I was just calling to let you know in case I was running a little late, but I should still be home on time." I told her that sounded like a great plan and to let me know when she was on the road and headed home. Then I told her I loved her and was proud of her for taking care of things, and reminded her to drive safely on the way home.

As I hung up the phone, I noticed my wife staring at me with a worried look on her face. She asked me if we should go down there to help. I told her that our daughter had it handled, and she would call us when she was on her way home. About twenty minutes later, I got a call from my daughter, letting me know she was on her way and everything was fine. My wife teared up and said she was so happy our daughter was as confident as she was and that she could handle these problems on her own.

What does this story say about my daughter? It tells me she is a confident problem solver, and courteous enough to let me know what is happening. It shows me that she knows how to take care of herself and work through a problem successfully.

Fathers need to help build confidence in their daughters by allowing them to work through problems and confrontations on their own. This can start right now. Allow your daughter to grow in confidence by showing her you believe in her. Even if she fails miserably, trust and have confidence in her, and don't stop letting her try.

Getting your wife on the same parenting plan is extremely important. If you are allowing your daughter to struggle through certain confrontations in order to grow, but your wife is constantly swooping in and rescuing her, this is very counterproductive parenting. Instead of growing, your daughter will always look to your wife to rescue her. Make sure you and your wife agree to allow your daughter to resolve confrontations on her own.

A parent's natural instinct is to rush in, fix the problem, and bask in the glory of being able to rectify any situation. Back off! This is not about you. This is about your daughter and teaching her that she is strong enough to get through anything in life on her own.

Imagine a professional boxer being trained for a fight. He learns how to keep his hands up, to protect himself at all times, to hit without being hit, to breathe properly, and so forth. Then the night of the big fight comes, and as the bell sounds for the first round to begin, the trainer jumps into the ring, pushes the boxer out of the way, and fights the fight for him! What is the point of training the fighter in the first place if he will never be allowed to practice what he has learned?

My daughter arrived home from school one day and explained that her teacher had given her a zero on a certain project for not turning an assignment in. My daughter had shown me the assignment before school, because she was proud of all the work she did on it, and she said she put it in the in-box on her teacher's desk before the class started. I would not have had to see the assignment myself to know that my daughter had done the work, but I just happened to know that she completed it on time and turned it in.

I listened as my daughter told me that her teacher was going to make her redo the assignment by the end of the week. It was a very big assignment, and my daughter had been working on it for at least a month. I asked her what she planned to do.

When something like this happens, most parents would jump right in, let the teacher know the assignment was completed, and demand justice. But I wanted to see how my daughter would handle this situation.

She told me that she tried talking to her teacher that day but could tell that the teacher was not having a good day because she kept telling my daughter to sit down and not to bother her. My daughter said that she would try to talk to her the next morning before school. She said she was not planning to do the assignment over since she had already done it.

When I got home from work the next day, I asked my daughter how things went at school. She told me she went up to her teacher and asked if she could speak with her for a minute. The teacher said she could. My daughter started off by saying that she knew without a doubt that she had not only completed the assignment but also put it in the teacher's in-box on her desk. My daughter said it was not fair of the teacher to ask her to do the project over again since she already did it and turned it in on time.

The teacher said she did not have it in her in-box and that she could either do the project over again or take the zero on it. My daughter tried to remain calm and asked if there was a possibility that the teacher may have moved it accidentally to another stack of papers. The teacher looked around on her desk and, while saying this was not possible, found the project my daughter had turned in.

The teacher apologized to my daughter for doubting her. She also applauded my daughter for standing her ground and speaking her mind.

These are the type of behaviors that we, as fathers, hope our daughters will exhibit. But the only way this will happen is if we allow our daughters to fight their own battles for as long as possible before offering any assistance. Even if our daughters ask us to step in and handle certain problems for them, it is our duty as fathers to encourage them to try their best to handle things on their own first.

When your daughter thinks she is fat or ugly, is too short or too tall, has too many pimples, or whatever, just listen. Then let her know that God made all different kinds of people, and since He is perfect and does not make mistakes, she must have been created perfectly, as well. Let her know that you think she is beautiful inside and out and that the people putting these ideas into her head are doing so only to make themselves feel superior.

Here's the trick: don't wait until your daughter has her confidence shaken to try to build it up. Letting your daughter know daily that she is all these wonderful things will keep negative thoughts at bay. That is not to say she will never feel this way, but knowing that you love and care for her, and that you think she is perfect just as she is, will mean more to her than anything that the jealous group of girls trying to make her feel bad about herself might say.

Does that mean you should lie to her about her appearance? Never! As fathers, we need to see the beauty in God's gift to us, both inside and out. It is also our job and our duty to make sure that our daughters see and understand that they are pure gifts from God.

This brings me to my favorite type of defense, the most important protection a daughter can receive from her father—spiritual protection. There is a constant spiritual battle for the souls of our daughters. A father's primary duty is to strengthen and empower his daughter to protect herself and fight against the enemy. Whether or not you believe a spiritual battle is happening does not change the fact that one is taking place, just as not believing in gravity doesn't make gravity any less real. You cannot see gravity, only the effects of it. The same is true with spiritual battles. It may not be so easy to see the actual battle happening, but the effects are obvious.

When I get home from work, I always ask my daughters to tell me about their day. Sometimes they tell me nothing important happened, which almost always means that they are thinking about and processing my question, and I need to wait a couple of minutes to get the real story about their day. Sometimes they burst into a story right away. Either way, I make asking them about their day a priority, and I look forward to hearing about whatever they tell me.

Countless times over the years, my daughters have told me about people getting picked on or made fun of at school, and how they stood up for those people, even if they really didn't like them.

Recently there was a scandalous rumor going around at my daughter's high school about a girl my daughter knew but really did not associate with. This girl basically had the entire school against her, saying awful things about her. Some kids told this girl she should kill herself! Some kids said they hoped she would die, and some others were so upset with her that they told other rumors about her and tried to destroy her on social media and behind her back at school.

My daughter sent me a text from school saying that just about everyone at her lunch table was trashing this girl's reputation and saying awful things, even people my daughter did not expect to think this way.

I asked my daughter how she felt about the rumors that were being spread. She said she wanted to stand up for this girl because even though she did not like her all that much, she did not think it was right for everyone to trash her reputation and say awful things about her.

I told her I knew she would do the right thing and that I would pray for her to gain the wisdom to make the right decisions on how to approach this angry crowd of trash-talking high school students. When I got home that evening, I asked her how the rest of her day had gone.

She said everyone was talking trash and saying mean things, and some even plotted to beat this girl up. So my daughter turned to one of the kids who was talking about the girl and told him, loudly enough for several people to hear, that the situation reminded her of Jesus protecting a woman from being stoned by telling the angry crowd that anyone who had not sinned was welcome to cast the first stone. The boy she had spoken to was a Christian, and she knew that her comment would have an effect on him. He stopped talking trash immediately and told her he had not considered that.

Another girl spoke up and said, "I don't care. I still want this girl to die." My daughter said, "That is not right, and if you were in her shoes, you would not want people to talk about you like this. It's wrong to want people to die. I understand you are upset, but you are taking it too far."

My daughter told me that most of the people at her table heard this exchange and got quiet. She said they stopped speaking badly about this girl and told her later that they were just upset and did not really mean the things they were saying.

My youngest daughter had a similar conversation with the people at her lunch table and stood up for this girl as well. Having courage like this comes from knowing right from wrong and not being afraid to speak up.

Confidence is the key here. My daughter had the confidence to stand up and fight against something she felt was not right, even though she did not hang out with the girl she was standing up for. That takes real courage. I know adults who would not have had the courage to do the same thing in that situation. I believe that this type of courage in standing up against what is wrong comes from years of encouragement and confidence building.

Encourage your daughter to try out for sports, join the marching band, or try out for a play or a dance team, or whatever she is interested in, so she can see how hard work and discipline pay off and empower her to be courageous. This will also let her know not to be afraid of trying and teach her how to fight for something she has set as a goal for herself.

Teach your daughter that she is more than just a physical being and that there is more to her than what she sees in the mirror. She will have a better understanding of what real beauty is and more confidence as well. Let your daughter know that since God made her in His image, she must be perfect in His eyes, just as she is perfect in your eyes. And always teach her to stand up and fight for what she believes in, no matter what!

TAKE ACTION

1. Teach your daughter how to fight. If you do not know how, find a video and learn from it—then teach your daughter. Show her how to punch, block, and move out of harm's way.

2. Teach your daughter to stand up for her beliefs—even if she is the only one doing so.
3. Let your daughter fight her own battles.
4. Teach your daughter that she does not have to conform to what the people around her believe.
5. Let your daughter know that spiritual attacks happen all the time, even if she is unaware of them. Encourage her to focus on God and fight for what she believes in.
6. Tell your daughter never to start a fight and never to run away from one if she has no other choice.
7. Lead by example.

CHALLENGE YOURSELF

Ask your daughter to pick a fight! Ask her to tell you about something she thinks is worth fighting for. Listen to what she has to say. Then challenge her to take a step toward fighting for what she believes in. For example, if your daughter thinks that the lunch served at her school is always stale and tastes awful, tell her to speak her mind. Let her know that she needs to put her words into actions, and encourage her to stand up for what she believes in. Whatever it is that she feels passionate about, encourage her not to be afraid to make her voice heard, even if she is the only one who feels this way.

Manly men take action—do this challenge now!

CHAPTER 4

TEACH HER MODESTY

Just by looking at the way advertisers attract young girls, it's easy to see that they are pushing the idea that more skin equals more attention. The clothing available to young girls can be very revealing and may send a message to boys that what they see is what they get. This can be a difficult message to make your daughter understand because it seems as though there are no other options for clothing.

The idea of women wearing immodest clothing and causing men to have certain thoughts is a discussion I have had with my daughters on several levels. On one hand, men are called to be responsible for their thoughts and to control their emotions; on the other hand, so are women. If a woman knows that wearing a bikini to church will cause certain reactions in others, she must also know that wearing revealing clothes can cause those same reactions in other locations.

It is our duty as manly men to let our daughters know that they are responsible for their choices. Our bodies are a gift from God and are not to be used carelessly. Teach your daughter to be sensitive to others' interpretations of the way she presents herself.

The key to teaching modesty is to lead by example. How does your wife dress? Do you encourage your wife to dress modestly, or do you always want her to show her body off? What sort of women does your daughter see you noticing and paying attention to? When you see a scantily clad woman on TV or in a movie, do you stare and make comments, either under your breath or out loud? Do you ogle women as they walk by you in the mall or on the street? Do you go to strip clubs, with or without your family's knowledge? What do your actions say about who you really are? As manly men, it is our responsibility to make our daughters aware of proper ways to dress, sit, walk, act, and so forth.

Popular culture tells young girls that there is nothing wrong with showing off their bodies. Advertisers use celebrities and popular "idols" to target young girls, who will rush to buy a product just because they want to be like the female pop star who endorses it.

In an old movie I watched on TV, a woman caused quite an uproar by wearing a swimsuit that exposed her legs. Her swimsuit was not revealing by any means compared with today's swimsuits, but for the era this movie was set in, the woman broke all the rules and got arrested for indecent exposure! It started me thinking about how much things have changed over time and what the future of fashion will look like for young girls. When it comes to fashion, hardly anything will be left to the imagination. It starts with clothing, but when there is hardly anything else to remove, it flows over into actions and personalities.

The word "modesty" is interpreted differently by different people. Modesty standards need to be set by the head of the household, the man of the house. Fatherly approval is very important to a daughter, and by helping your daughter to understand that you do not approve of immodest clothing and behavior, you will guide her toward things you do approve of. By teaching this behavior to your daughter, you set healthy boundaries and expectations for her to follow.

TEACH HER MODESTY

SUCCESS STORY

I had a conversation about modesty with my oldest daughter as she was preparing to enter high school. She had gone to a Catholic grade school and had worn a school uniform. The uniform was very modest, and the other clothes my daughter owned were in line with the modest clothes she wore at school.

Now she would be entering a public high school—no more uniforms! This presented an opportunity for me to go shopping with her to pick out clothes for school.

We entered the first clothing store in the mall on a Saturday morning to find it full of girls my daughter's age who, like us, were shopping for school clothes. On the first rack of clothes I passed was a pair of shorts that could not have been more than five inches from the top of the waistline to the bottom of the legs, where they were cut with a jagged edge. "Low-rise cutoff jean shorts," the label said. I put a pair of them on my head and asked my daughter how she liked my new headband. She laughed, told me to take them off my head immediately, and giggled as she walked to another rack of clothes, pretending she hardly knew me.

I started seeing a pattern in the clothes the store offered. The shirts were tiny and mostly see-through, the shorts had barely enough material on them to be called shorts, and there were a ton of images all over the place showing how these clothes looked on models whose bodies were barely contained by the clothes they were wearing.

I asked my daughter if she wanted to go to another store to check out the clothes there instead. She told me that all the stores would be offering the same general style of clothes. I asked her if she saw anything wrong with the clothes that were being sold there, and she said that all the kids were wearing things like this, and it was normal.

She said that there was no law against wearing short shorts and that if people looked at someone wearing clothes like this and treated her any differently, it was not the problem of the person wearing the clothes; it was the problem of the person looking at the girl wearing the clothes, she insisted.

I asked her if she thought it was responsible for someone to dress immodestly and not to expect a certain reaction. She said that it should not matter what someone is wearing, only who they are inside.

As impressed as I was with her train of thought, I felt she was missing something. I kept asking questions to see if I could get her to see what I was seeing. I asked her if her statement applied to everyone, including me. She said it did.

I asked her how she would feel if I went into the dressing room and tried on a pair of those shorts. She stared at me for a second, not able to tell whether I was being serious. Fearing I was serious, she said, "Dad, please don't." I said, "Why not?" She said that people would stare at me and think I was a sicko or a pervert or something like that.

I said, "I am confused. I thought you said it was not the problem of the person wearing the clothes. I thought you said it was the people looking at the person wearing certain clothes who had the problem?" I added, "I know who I am on the inside, and that is all that should matter, right?"

She said, "Okay, let's go to another store. I get the point." Then she laughed at the image in her head of me wearing those tiny shorts.

We sat on the bench in the middle of the mall, just outside the store we were just in, and talked. I knew what she was trying to say; I just wanted her to know what she was actually saying. I have found that allowing my daughters to come to their own conclusion through self-realization is better than trying to tell them something. It's a sweet science that takes time to get right. I asked her to consider why girls would wear revealing clothing. She pondered that question for a minute and said, "Maybe to get attention." I pushed her thinking further by asking why they felt they might need attention. My daughter said they were probably missing out on that attention from somewhere else and wanted to feel as if someone noticed them. She had come to the realization that not only does what you wear send a message to those around you, but there is usually a reason that message is being sent, whether intentional or not.

I asked her if she thought that wearing revealing clothing showed a lack of confidence in these girls. My daughter said she did not directly connect the lack of confidence with dressing a certain way at first but that she could see my point.

My goal was not necessarily to get my daughter to agree with me completely but only to see my point. I was not asking her to dress completely covered from head to toe but to consider that modesty can be even more attractive than showing everything off.

We went into several stores that day looking for modest clothes, but I was not the one being picky about the choices. My daughter would bring clothes into the dressing room, try them on, and then come out with an armful of clothes for the "no" pile and a few for the "yes" pile. I asked her why she chose the outfits she chose, and she said she thought they best represented who she was and she did not want to send the wrong message about herself.

This type of father-daughter relationship takes time to cultivate. Being honest and understanding with your daughter can help reach this goal. I cannot honestly say that my kids never lied to me or that I was always right with the choices I made concerning them, but I can honestly say that everything was done with a great deal of love and care, always with their best interests in mind.

When your daughter comes out of her room wearing something that you consider less than modest, don't ignore it because you are worried about getting into an argument with her. Don't get upset and start an argument either. The right way to address it is to let her know that you are not okay with the choice she made for her clothing and to ask her to change into something more appropriate.

When you ask your daughter to do something like this, she will more than likely have a problem with it, so expect some resistance. That does not mean you should change your mind. As a father, you must have clear instructions at all times for your daughter. If you told her to go change, expect her to get back in her room and change.

Once she has followed your request, you can sit down with her and explain your reasoning. Do not expect her to agree with you or your reasons; expect her only to follow your requests without argument. The fact that you are taking the time to help her understand your reasoning does not mean she has to agree with you by the end of your discussion. You are planting seeds in your daughter's mind. It can take a while for those seeds to grow.

I told my daughter that I was proud of her for listening to me and following my rules even though she did not agree with me. I asked her to trust that I was doing this only for her best interests.

My daughter said she trusted me but still disagreed on a few of the restrictions I placed on her dress. I asked her if I had ever done anything to make her look bad or to hurt her in any way. She said no. I said, "Okay, just think about that for a minute. Everything I do is because I love you and want the best for you."

Being manly means having rules you are able to explain clearly to your daughter. She does not have to agree with your rules; she has only to follow them and know that you will always have her best interests in mind. Try to avoid the phrase "because I said so." Unfortunately, this response seems to come naturally to most parents.

Create clear rules for your daughter and know why you have set them so it will be easy to explain them when you are questioned. Again, this does not mean that your daughter will understand or agree with your reasons for having these rules; she just needs to know that everything you do has her best interests in mind and that you would never do anything to harm her in any way.

TAKE ACTION

1. Use caution with the types of TV shows you watch with your daughter. What are these shows showing her about modesty?
2. Discuss your daughter's favorite celebrity or music group with her, and have her tell you what she thinks about their views on modesty.
3. Make sure your daughter understands that she is more than a physical being.
4. Stick to your rules about clothing and help your daughter adapt these rules for herself by being understanding and patient.

5. Lead by example. If you have a bikini-model calendar but expect your daughter to dress modestly, you are fooling yourself. She will pick up on the type of women you take notice of.

CHALLENGE YOURSELF

Your challenge—if you feel you are manly enough—is to ask your daughter to go through her closet and pull out one outfit she feels is too revealing or immodest. Tell her she has two options: to give the outfit away to charity or to find a way to make the outfit more modest. If the shirt is too revealing, maybe she can find another shirt to wear over it. Let her work this out on her own and find a resolution, but stick with it and challenge your daughter to think about her modesty.

Manly men take action—do this challenge now!

CHAPTER 5

SHUT UP AND LISTEN

There is a huge difference between hearing and listening. I have heard it said that people hear with their ears but listen with their mind. When your daughter speaks to you, you have a choice: are you going to hear her, or are you going to listen to her?

When you actively listen, you take in what someone is saying, try to understand it, repeat it back, and ask questions to gain better understanding.

Most girls like to talk. They need to communicate their feelings. That's why there are many, many more journals purchased by women than by men. The nice thing about a journal is that it does not talk back; it just listens without judgment or consequence. Whether or not your daughter chooses to speak with you depends on how approachable you are.

There will be times when your daughter will need to tell you something without fear that you will offer advice before she is finished speaking or try to fix the problem for her.

That's where the trouble begins. As men, we like to fix things. I believe it is a natural instinct that makes us act this way. Men like to let everyone know that they don't need instructions, that they already know the answer to any question life throws at them, and that, no, they don't have a problem changing a tire on their own without the assistance of a roadside auto service.

For some reason, men find it very difficult to sit and listen. When my daughter is telling me about something that she's having a hard time with, I find it difficult at times not to cut her off and offer advice or a solution to fix her problem. As fathers of daughters, we are always going to be faced with situations that require us simply to listen and process the information internally. Even if you can process information extremely quickly, it is important to let it sink in before you blurt out a remedy.

One such time will be when your daughter is crying over a relationship issue, whether it is with her best friend or a boy she thinks is cute but does not even know she exists. There will be times when nothing you can possibly say will help the situation immediately. So just listen! Then ask questions to help you understand exactly what she means.

I like to offer something for my daughters to think about when one of these problems arises, so this particular piece of advice is difficult for me to adhere to—but I do my best!

MY FAILURE

One situation that I consider a big failure on my part was when my middle daughter was having a hard time with her high school basketball team.

I have a rule for my daughters: if you begin something, you must finish it. I believe that this rule teaches perseverance and commitment, as well as discipline and self-control. My daughter had been playing basketball since kindergarten and became very skilled at it. She was on several travel teams in an AAU league and had played on various competitive teams since the sixth grade.

When she got to high school, she was surrounded with a group of girls who were extremely toxic. Just about all of them smoked pot, drank alcohol, and were sexually active—with one another. My daughter did not want to be part of this crowd, as she had been raised to avoid these types of situations and people. Being a very skilled player and having a great personality, she was made the captain of her team. She came home and told me the news about the coach having chosen her as captain but was worried because she really did not like the girls on her team. Those girls did not like her either and took every opportunity to let her know that. She knew she had to try to bond with them to be a good team leader, but that would be difficult.

After a few weeks, she told me that she was not enjoying playing on this team and that she really did not want to be around these girls any longer.

I told her that she should not give up on playing basketball because of her teammates. I told her she would need to know how to handle adversity and overcome being around, and in charge of, people who did not get along with her. I basically told her that this was an opportunity to work through something difficult and learn to resolve a conflict.

She stayed with the team through her sophomore year in high school and into her junior year. The coach became very tough on my daughter and would yell at her and blame her for things that other people were doing wrong. Since none of her teammates liked her anyway, they never stood up to take the blame; instead they let the consequences fall on my daughter.

She told me she was having problems with her coach more than ever this year. She understood the difference between being yelled *to* and being yelled *at* in sports and that having a tough coach did not necessarily mean the coach had anything against her. She understood that sometimes coaches try to pull the best efforts out of the best players by being more critical of them than anyone else on the team. She understood all these things, but she still recognized that the coach's treatment of her was way over the top.

She asked what I thought she should do, and again I told her she should try to talk to the coach. She told me she already did, but I told her to try again and to reason with him in a one-on-one setting. I assumed that she had not been catching the coach at the right time to speak with him and suggested she try talking to him either before or after practice, when all the other girls were gone.

She tried at least a dozen times to speak to her coach about the issues she was having with the team and about his treatment of her. He never listened. He never even tried to process what she was telling him into something he could work with. He was, and is, a very stubborn man.

I thought to myself, "Thank goodness I am not like this coach!" I heard what my daughter said about not liking basketball anymore, right? Wasn't I just trying to help her stay committed to her sport? I had to help her stay on the team because, in my mind, that was the only way for her to learn a lesson about perseverance — or at least I thought what I was doing was right.

While I thought I was listening to what she was saying, I was only hearing what I wanted to hear. I did not take time to ask questions to find out how she was feeling deep down.

My daughter did not want to play basketball any longer. She lost her passion for playing the sport she once loved and was becoming very unhappy. For whatever reason, I apparently did not want to hear what she was saying. I should have taken the time to ask deeper questions and spent my time listening to my daughter instead of simply hearing what she was saying. I was treating her more like a first-round draft pick than my daughter. In reality, I was worse than this coach. This was my own daughter, and I was so caught up in teaching her a lesson about not quitting that I completely failed to listen to what she was saying. I did not ask her any questions about what she thought she should do; I only offered advice. Unfortunately, my advice was based on what I thought I would do in this situation, not what I thought would be best for her.

I saw my daughter as a basketball star and saw a future for her playing in college and possibly beyond. This hope I had for her did not take her feelings into consideration. I thought only of the lesson I was trying to teach her and how I viewed her future playing basketball. Subconsciously, I was forcing her to live my dream for her future.

I found out that she was depressed about her situation with the team. She hated going to practice, hated playing basketball, and started to feel trapped. I noticed that she was unhappy quite a bit and had a serious talk with her to find out what was happening.

She brought up her basketball situation again and said she felt as though I really did not understand how much she hated playing. She said she had been absolutely miserable for the past two or three years, since she had been around these girls and her coach, and it made her not want to play the game at all anymore.

FINALLY — SUCCESS

Finally, I listened. I asked my daughter what she wanted to do. She said she was not sure. She said she did not want to disappoint me. I asked her a lot of questions to find out not only how she felt, but to see if she could walk me through the reasons she was feeling this way. I asked her if she wanted to quit the team.

I had asked her that before, but this time was different. In the past, I would say, "So, what do you want to do about it, quit the team?" But I would apparently have a tone of disappointment in my voice, because my daughter would always respond with "No."

I could see that she was sad. This was different from practicing tough love and making her work through a difficult situation. She was playing only to make me happy. I needed to make sure I put her feelings first and to make her know that I meant what I said.

I said, "If you do not want to play anymore, I completely understand. I am not disappointed in you, and I do not think you are a quitter. I am here for you, and I want you to be happy. I suggest that you pray about your decision and think it through with your heart and let me know what you decide. But either way, I will always love you and support whatever decision you make."

For the first time, I saw her look a little less stressed, and I noticed that she was considering what was best for her instead of trying not to disappoint me. She put real thought and prayer into it and then told me that she had decided that the next game would be her last. She said she was tired of being manipulated by this coach and used as a scapegoat. She was tired of being forced to hang around people she felt were toxic to her, and she planned on letting her coach know exactly why she was quitting the team.

She told me all of this with a tear in her eye. I noticed her becoming emotional and gave her a big hug. She said that she never wants to disappoint me or my wife and that she did not want to be thought of as a quitter. I told my daughter that she was not a quitter and that anyone who can remove herself from a toxic situation, instead of continuing to be mistreated, was a winner, not a loser. I told her that she would never be able to do anything that would make me stop loving her and that I would never be disappointed in her.

I asked her if there was any other sport that she wanted to try or anything else that she had been unable to do because of her relentless, time-consuming basketball schedule. She answered that she had always been interested in Brazilian jiu-jitsu and would like to take lessons. I told her that I would support her in anything she really felt a passion for. I also told her to make sure it was something she wanted to do, not something to make anyone else happy. She assured me that this would be for her and her alone. For Christmas, I got her a membership at a local jiu-jitsu gym, and she was very excited to receive it and give it a try.

I asked her the other day if she was happy with her decision to quit playing basketball, or if she missed the game. She thought for a minute and said, "Absolutely not—I don't miss anything about the game, the people I was surrounded with, or the coach I had!" She said even if she had a different team and coach, she would not want to play anymore.

This time I listened and said, "As long as you are happy, I am fine with whatever you want to do."

That can be a dangerous statement to make to your daughter if she does not have God in her life, because her decisions will not necessarily be based on good moral thinking. If, however, God is always included in the decisions your daughter makes, you can be sure that she is making sound decisions based on high moral standards, instead of "feel good now" choices.

The best thing that came out of this situation with my daughter was when I apologized to her for not listening to what she was telling me. I told her I failed and was sorry. I made sure to correct my mistakes and to try my best to listen to all of my daughters whenever they want to talk.

The honesty that comes from letting your daughter know you are sorry for not listening and that you failed can take your relationship with her to a much deeper level.

I thought I had this fathering thing figured out—I guess not! If you expect to be perfect as a father, your daughter will expect to be perfect as a daughter. There is no possible way perfection can be reached by any human, but that does not mean we should plan to fail. It means only that when we do fail, we need to be honest with ourselves, be aware of the failure, and do our best to correct our actions in the future.

Being able to have an honest discussion with your daughter, to ask her for forgiveness, and to move forward is essential for a successful father-daughter relationship. When was the last time you apologized to your daughter for something? Have you ever told her you failed at something? Maybe it's time to let her know you are sorry. You might be surprised at the discussions that follow if you listen to what she has to say.

There is always time for giving advice, but you have to understand completely what your daughter is saying before you can offer advice.

TAKE ACTION

1. Give your daughter time to process and think about what she is saying—then listen carefully!

2. Practice active listening—ask questions about what your daughter tells you.
3. Do not interrupt your daughter when she is speaking. Expect the same from her when you speak.
4. Try to understand what your daughter is telling you by repeating it back to her and asking if you got it right.
5. Don't assume that your daughter is thinking a certain way—ask her to clarify her feelings and express herself.
6. Speak the truth to your daughter at all times. If she hears you speak the truth, she will do the same.
7. Let your daughter know if you are wrong. Swallow your pride. Which is more important: your pride or your daughter?
8. Apologize if you are wrong or have hurt your daughter's feelings.

CHALLENGE YOURSELF

Your challenge is in two parts.

1. Ask your daughter about her day, and then—without being judgmental, without offering any instant-fix-it advice, and without interrupting her in any way—listen to what she tells you. Ask questions based on what she tells you, instead of questions you already have in your mind. This lets her know you are truly listening.
2. Ask your daughter if there is anything you have done to upset her or make her angry. If there is, apologize

to her sincerely. Let her know you only have her best interests in mind, and you will do your best always to put her feelings first.

Manly men take action—do this challenge now!

CHAPTER 6

Prepare Her for Boyfriends and Beyond

Just when you think you have things figured out as a dad and start to hit a groove in your parenting, God sees you being too comfortable and reckons it's time for you to grow once again. Out of pain and discomfort, God helps us grow. I am convinced this is the reason He created boyfriends!

Shut your eyes for a second and think about your daughter. Imagine she has become interested in boys and wants to start dating. She knows the type of man you are and how you treat women. She knows everything about you, even the things that are private and secret and you think no one knows. Your daughter knows and understands the real you.

Now imagine that she comes home from school one day and tells you that she found a boy who is exactly like you and she is interested in dating him. Open your eyes. Are you happy, or are you very concerned with her choice? Have you stopped breathing completely at the thought of this actually happening? You may want to keep your eyes shut and hope to wake up from the nightmare you are currently having. If you are not completely thrilled with her choice, you may need to change some things about yourself and start becoming manly.

My oldest daughter was a junior in high school before she had a real boyfriend. She had gone to the movies with a group of boys and girls several times as friends and sat next to the boy she liked, but he was not a boyfriend with whom she would spend any real time.

All that changed one day when she came home from school yelling, "Guess what? A boy in my class just asked me to go to the movies with him this weekend. I am so excited! I really like this boy, and I was hoping he would ask me out." She had never been on an actual date.

"And so it begins," I thought. When my daughter told me about the boy asking her on a date, immediately my mind started plotting scare tactics. How could I intimidate this boy to make sure he treated my daughter with respect?

Does this boy know I can crush a coconut with my bare hands? Does he know that I have never lost a fight, and I am not about to let him start disrespecting my daughter? What about showing him some scars I have and telling him how I got them? That would scare him for sure! I imagined myself sitting on the couch in a tank top, cleaning my guns and sharpening my knives as this boy arrived to take my daughter on a date.

Wait a second! What was I worried about? I raised my daughter to make good choices, right? Did I tell her everything she needed to know about boys, everything she needed to be aware of, and what boys are really like? I started thinking back to every conversation we ever had about boys and girls, the birds and the bees, keeping high moral standards, and so forth.

Then I started thinking about the type of person my daughter had become. She was actively involved in church, talked to me all the time about problems, asked for advice, and had a great relationship with me. So why was I so worried about this boy-friend situation? How different could life be now that she was interested in a boy?

I started to imagine her yelling things like, "You just don't love me like he does!" and, "You don't understand the love I have for him!" I was terrifying myself! The emotional roller-coaster ride had begun. I was losing my mind and trying to keep my cool at the same time. She had barely come into the house to tell me the whole story, and I was already having all these thoughts. I took a deep breath and asked her to tell me what happened. She went through her story about how he asked her, exactly what he said, how she reacted, what her best friend thought, and so forth.

She told me that he wanted to go to a movie with her on the weekend and asked if it was okay. I told her it was fine and asked what movie they were planning on seeing. She told me the name of the movie, which happened to be rated R. It was a war movie, not overtly sexual or vulgar, but there was quite a bit of shooting, and so forth. It was a war movie after all! I told her I trusted her and said she could go.

When the weekend came, I drove her to the theater to meet this boy and walked her to the door. The boy said hello and greeted me. He said he was going to get the tickets and would be right back. My daughter said, "Okay, Dad, you can go now!" I just laughed at her and said I would be leaving in a minute. When the boy returned, he said he was not old enough to buy tickets for an R-rated movie and said they would have to see another movie. He said that someone over seventeen had to be in the theater with them for them to see the movie.

I said I would get the tickets for them and watch the movie as well. Instantly, my daughter shot me a wide-eyed stare, and I could swear that this boy had turned into a pillar of salt. I told them both not to worry, as I was only going to buy the tickets for them, then I would just sit between them and hold the popcorn, so they could both reach their snack while we watched the movie!

Obviously I was kidding, but I am not sure the boy took a breath again until we all got into the theater and he realized I was not going to sit with them. I sat toward the middle of the theater, and my daughter and her date sat a few rows behind me.

Jokingly, I told my middle daughter that I would be going on her first date with her as well, which was also to the movies. She said she sort of expected it and did not mind. I really wanted to see the movie that she and her date were planning to see anyway, so I went in and sat apart from them, as I had with my first daughter, and watched the movie. By the time my youngest daughter was asked on her first date, also to the movies, I figured it was a tradition and just went with the flow!

I know a lot of fathers who forbid their daughters to date until a certain age. I honestly feel that if you instill a sense of confidence in your daughter when she is young, she will not feel the "need" to have a boy in her life until she is mature enough to handle dating. Therefore, I never told my daughters that they could not date until they reached a certain age.

If you decide to use this approach to dating with your daughter, you must be present in her life at all times. If you are not involved actively in her life, she will find another boy to take your place. This is where a lot of problems can begin.

RESPECT YOUR WIFE

Men need to set an example for their daughters to show them how a man is supposed to treat a woman. This example needs to start with how men treat their wives. If you treat your wife with respect, your daughter will expect to be treated the same way by her boyfriends. If you put your wife down and disrespect her, your daughter will end up with boys who treat her the same way because she thinks this is the way it is supposed to be.

Your daughter notices everything about you as a man. She sees how you act toward women in front of your wife and behind your wife's back. She can tell if you are walking through the mall with her and start staring at a woman's body as she walks past you. Your daughter can tell what type of man you are and how you view women's roles in the family by the remarks you make about women.

If you think a woman's place is on a stripper pole, be prepared to see your daughter on one someday. If you want to become familiar with the term "baby daddy," keep treating your wife with disrespect and your daughter will end up with the type of man who uses her for his own gratification and leaves her to fend for herself.

If, instead, you are respectful, hold your wife in high regard, bring her flowers, and treat her like a lady, your daughter will eventually find a man who does the same for her. Your wife and daughter need to see you as the head of your family. You need to be the head of your family, and God expects you to be in charge. Be the type of man you want your daughter to marry.

THREE LESSONS IN DATING

Years ago, when people who know me would ask how I planned on dealing with having three daughters dating at the same time, I would respond with, "I'm not worried. Nuns don't date!" Although becoming a nun is not out of the question for any of my daughters, my response was mainly my joking way of not thinking about their dating anyone.

Dealing with relationships between your daughter and her boyfriend can be difficult if you are not prepared. I have come up with a few things I consider very helpful that might just help you survive the dating years with some hair left over on your head!

1. *Teach your daughter to keep her relationship in perspective.* It's easy for young dating couples to get caught up in their relationship and become self-absorbed. Help your daughter to keep things in perspective — it's not the end of the world if she does not get to see her boyfriend for one day, and they should not be fighting and bickering all the time with one another. They are young; they need to have fun and laugh. Teach your daughter to take healthy doses of time away from her boyfriend to spend time with her friends and family.

2. *Restrict alone time.* A good rule for your daughter is never to be completely alone with her boyfriend. I know that sounds a bit crazy, but believe me, it works. A friend of mine who has been married for over twenty years told me that he and his wife avoided tempting situations when they were dating by promising never to be alone with each other, whether in a parked car, in an apartment, in a house, or wherever. They always had family or friends with them whenever they went anywhere together. I thought this was a great idea and shared this story with my daughters. There is no reason for your daughter to put herself in a tempting situation if there is a way to avoid it in the first place.

3. *Keep an eye on how touchy-feely they are.* It's natural for boys and girls to be attracted to one another sexually.

This is probably not what you want to hear right now, especially when you're thinking about your daughter and her boyfriend, but it's true. If they are sitting on the couch together, keep an eye on their hands and their postures. Although having sexual feelings in a dating relationship is normal, it does not mean that those feelings must be acted on. There is no reason for your daughter and her boyfriend to be lying all over each other. Your daughter needs to know how to set boundaries for her boyfriend to respect. If he feels that he can get away with anything he wants and allow his hands to roam anywhere he likes, he will. Teach her to set boundaries now.

It is one thing for you to point these things out to your daughter, but it is more important that she set these boundaries herself and demand that her boyfriend respect them. If you are not talking with your daughter about her relationship with her boyfriend, she may be getting advice from her friends or another less-than-reliable source. How can your daughter ever know what your expectations are if you don't talk to her about them?

My best friend always says, "Arousal is spousal," meaning that being aroused sexually should be saved for your spouse someday. Letting things get out of hand can happen very quickly, and your daughter needs to know that she is in control of herself and is able to stop any advancement that puts her integrity into question.

A GREAT STORY

Here is a story I would like to tell you before we continue. There was a farmer who raised lambs. He had a large farm and tried his best to protect the lambs from wolves living in the nearby countryside. One day he shot a wolf that was trying to kill one of his lambs and found out that she had recently given birth.

He felt awful for shooting the wolf, but he had to protect his lambs, so he took the wolf pup in and raised it to be a pet. The wolf was well trained and very docile. The farmer trained it to protect the lambs on the farm and keep the other wolves away. As it grew larger, the farmer grew to trust the wolf more.

One day the farmer had to go to town, and instead of tying up the wolf, as he usually did, he let it run free so that it could protect the lambs. When the farmer returned from town, he found the wolf standing over a lamb it had just killed. The farmer was upset with the wolf and started yelling at it, saying, "How could you do this? I trusted you and you broke my trust!" The wolf looked at the man and said (in this story the wolf talks—just go with it), "What did you expect from me? I am a wolf, and this is my nature!"

I know we are talking about a wolf in the story above, and not a boy or a girl, but there are certain human instincts that are not fair to test constantly. Avoiding tempting situations is not only a good practice for men to teach their daughters; it is a good to practice for them to follow as well.

WARNING SIGNS

No relationship is perfect. There will always be arguments and disagreements, especially in a new relationship. That's normal. In fact, disagreements can offer an opportunity for your daughter and her boyfriend to become closer as they work through resolving a conflict together. In all relationships, however, there are warning signs that your daughter needs to be aware of. Here are some guidelines to share with your daughter as she starts her dating years:

1. *Avoid boys who flatter.* Flattery can be a sign of manipulation and a way for boys to reach their "goal."
2. *Avoid boys who give many gifts.* This type of boy can be trying to set up a sort of "exchange" system. "I gave you a necklace, so you owe me."
3. *Avoid thin-skinned boys.* Boys who are easily offended can try to use girls as a scapegoat for their problems, to make themselves feel better.
4. *Avoid boys who think they are never wrong.* This type of boy will eventually cause you to feel as if everything you do is wrong, and this can break your confidence.
5. *Avoid rude and disrespectful boys.* There is no reason to stay with a person who refuses to be respectful and to value you as a person.
6. *Avoid self-centered boys.* Any boy who is more concerned with his appearance than with you is surely too self-absorbed to concentrate on you.
7. *Avoid boys whom your family and friends do not like.* Your family has your best interests in mind—listen to them! Their intuition is usually right on the money, and they will be able to see things happening in your relationship that you fail to see.
8. *Avoid boys with anger issues.* Even if the anger is not directed toward you yet, one day it will be!
9. *Avoid liars and cheaters.* No second chances: if this boy lied or cheated once, there will be a second time and a third. Do not be an enabler.

10. *Avoid overbearing and controlling boys.* If your boy-friend sticks to you like a leech, and gets angry, sad, or hurt when you want to spend time with your friends or without him, run! He is too needy, and you don't need that! Often these boys have very few friends of their own—for a good reason!

11. *Avoid boys for whom you have to make excuses.* If you are apologizing for your boyfriend now, you will always be apologizing for him. Don't make excuses for his actions or inactions.

12. *Never date a boy who is physically abusive.* Any boy who lays an angry hand on a woman is not a real man and does not need to be with a woman at all.

13. *Never chase a boy.* Never follow a boy around like a lost puppy. You should not be a convenience for him whenever he feels like seeing you; his time for you must be intentional.

It's easy for your daughter to let her heart make decisions in her relationships. Adults do this all the time. The problem is that the heart does not understand warning signs. It's important to use your head when making decisions about relationships. If you can teach your daughter to work through issues with her head instead of with her heart, you are off to a good start.

It is our duties as fathers to make sure our daughters know what type of treatment they should expect from men and can recognize mistreatment. When a father empowers his daughter this way, he is setting her up for a future full of happiness instead of sadness. Lead by example and show your daughter how a man should treat a woman by treating your wife with respect and honor.

FATHER–DAUGHTER DATES

Being manly means making time to take your daughter on father-daughter dates. Find something to do that allows good conversation to happen between the two of you. Sitting in a movie theater together and watching a movie is not a horrible idea, but it does not allow for much conversation to take place. Make time each day to listen to your daughter, and at least twice a month, take your daughter on a date.

You don't have to spend a lot of money. You do not have to go to expensive restaurants or do elaborate things. Even walking through the park; having a picnic; playing checkers, cards, or chess; or just sitting and looking at the sunset are ways to spend valuable time with your daughter. Treating her this way is indicative of how she will expect other men throughout her life to treat her.

Spending time is more important than spending money. If you asked your daughter what her fondest memories are, I'll bet they would have to do with family time during a vacation or with an experience she had, rather than with a gift she received. She will remember things you do together more than the gifts you buy her. Make time to spend time together.

When it comes to spending time with your daughter, the most important bit of advice I can offer is to *put your phone down*! Be present to your daughter. The time you spend with her now is important to her. She needs to know that you are interested in her and in her life.

The men your daughter chooses to be with must be held to this level of expectation, so that she won't settle for a "feel good now" partner who couldn't care less about her and her future.

Girls need fathers who are involved in their daily lives. They need dads who are willing to sacrifice their own selfish desires and put aside material things to provide what their daughters need. Girls need a hero to look up to. If someone asked your daughter who her hero is, would your name come up first? Would your name come up at all?

Is your wife proud of the type of man you are? Women need to be proud of their husbands, and they need to let their daughters know they should expect the same type of man for themselves in the future. It's never too late to become the type of man your wife is proud of.

TAKE ACTION

1. Treat your daughter with respect at all times. Never let her be disrespected.
2. Lead by example: treat your wife with respect.
3. Take your wife on dates.
4. Take your daughter on father-daughter dates.
5. Be a hero to your daughter.
6. Put your phone down and be present to your family whenever they need your attention.

CHALLENGE YOURSELF

Lead by example. This is a two-part challenge.

1. Bring your wife flowers and candy. That's right! Start teaching your daughter to expect kindness from her future spouse by the way you treat your wife.

2. Take your daughter on a date and bring her flowers as well. You and your daughter should spend time getting to know each other. Take a walk in a park, watch the sunset, play cards, paint something together—anything to spend quality time with each other.

Manly men take action—do this challenge now!

CHAPTER 7

Eat Meals Together

I come from an Italian family that loves to eat! Growing up, I always looked forward to holiday meals because my whole family would be seated together, stuffed into the modest dining room at my grandparents' house. I never knew what to expect from a big family meal. Would it involve nonstop laughter, a huge argument, a discussion about politics, an in-depth discussion about religion, or all of the above?

During our family meals, no matter what the topic of discussion was, everyone got in on it and always had something to say. From the youngest at the table to the oldest, we all spoke our mind, and every voice was listened to.

Looking back at the meals my family shared, I see how important they were in forming the person I am today. I learned how to speak my mind and to stand up for what I believed in, even when not everyone agreed with me; how to resolve conflict; how to begin each meal with a prayer of thanks to God; and how to find laughter in just about every subject.

Today, the importance of eating meals together as a family has been almost completely forgotten. Instead of spending quality time together and having deep conversations, families seem to be distracted by their electronic devices. I am always baffled by the rudeness of people who sit across the table from each other and then ignore each other and stare at their phones. It's almost as if people would rather be with those whose lives they are snooping at online than the persons sitting across from them.

Families are starved of time together. It's a manly responsibility to make sure your family is being fed—not only with food, but with quality time as well. The family dinner table is meant to be a place where families can discuss, de-stress, and lean on one another for support. Dinnertime is a time for families to relax, laugh with one another, hear interesting things that happened during the day, debate with one another, and basically feel recharged.

Family meals used to be sacred times. Growing up, I remember getting a busy signal anytime I called a friend's house near dinnertime. That usually meant that my friend's family were eating dinner and not to bother them until dinner was finished. I knew families who would not even get up to answer the door if someone rang their doorbell while they were eating together. Mealtime is family time, and nothing comes before that.

It can be this way again. It's a manly job to take on, but there are ways to get your family to look forward to mealtime together.

MEALTIME RULES

1. *Turn the television off.* It doesn't matter if the conversation is so boring that you would rather sew your head to the carpet than listen to a family member drone on; do your best to focus on the conversation. What is there on television that could possibly be more important than spending time with your family? Oh, you

are watching the news to find out whether it's raining? Try opening a window and looking outside. No excuses—turn the TV off!

2. *Leave your phone in another room, and insist that your family do the same.* Your daughter doesn't need to know which of her friends sent her a message during family mealtime. In the same respect, you do not need to know if your office called, sent a text, or even sent you an e-mail. The score from the game you are watching can wait, too. Leave the phones in another room, and be present to one another.

3. *Start dinner with a prayer.* Say a prayer of thanks to God for the food you are about to eat and for your family's being together. This teaches your daughter to keep God first in all things.

4. *Talk to one another during and after your meal.* Talk about what happened during your day. Ask your daughter and your wife about their day. Tell them about your day after they tell you about theirs—put them first!

In preschool, my oldest daughter learned a prayer before meals that my family still uses:

Thank You for the world so sweet; thank You for the food we eat; thank You for the birds that sing; thank You, God, for everything!

My family started a tradition when my daughter brought this mealtime prayer home. I was so proud of her for learning it and teaching it to the family that, after we said the prayer, I gave her a high five and told her she did a great job. The next night at dinner, after the prayer, she reached over and gave me a high five, and from then on, we have kept up the tradition of high-fiving each other after our mealtime prayer.

As time went on, this became very natural to my family as part of our prayer. One night, my daughter had a friend spend the night at our house, and after we had prayed before dinner, we all reached out and gave each other high fives. My wife started laughing because my daughter's friend was looking at us as if we were crazy. "What was that all about?" she asked. Then we all started laughing and explained it to her. Later we found out that my daughter's friend started saying this prayer with her own family.

Whenever my daughters' friends are at our house for a meal, they never bring their phones to the table, as they are aware of my rules. They seem to look forward to being away from their phones and having good old face-to-face communication. It's strange at first for some of these girls because they are not used to communicating without their phones, but having face-to-face communication is extremely important and builds character as well as confidence.

There have been times when my daughters' friends were over for dinner and were shocked to see my whole family sit, pray, and eat together at the table without the television on and without anyone bringing their phone to the table. On these occasions, my daughter's friends seem to want to sit and talk for hours at the dinner table. Sadly, these girls are not experiencing this type of interaction with their own families, and they desperately need it.

The dinner table is absolutely no place for phones. People allow phones to rob them of important family time. It's not just kids spending too much time on their phones either; parents have become so self-absorbed that they have forgotten what is really important in life—family time.

BENEFITS OF FAMILY MEALTIME

There are many benefits of family mealtime.

1. *It builds self-esteem.* Showing your daughter that she is important enough to set time aside for each day will help build her self-esteem.

2. *It encourages conflict resolution.* Eating reduces stress and relaxes most people, so mealtime is a great time to resolve conflicts with one another in a peaceful setting.

3. *It creates a sense of belonging.* Just knowing that your family waits for you before they start eating will build a strong family foundation. The sense of "team" is important to convey the message that you have your family's back and they have yours.

4. *It keeps God first.* Making a habit of praying together before meals carries over into all other aspects of life and shows that God comes first in all things.

5. *It teaches your family about sacrifice.* Make a point of never filling your plate before your family have their plates full. Allowing your family to help themselves first brings them to understand that you are concerned that they have enough to eat. This unspoken gesture resonates deeper than words alone and shows your family your priorities.

6. *It opens the lines of communication.* Letting your daughter know that she has a set time of day to speak with her family about problems, or to share exciting news, establishes a sense of security and healthy communication patterns within the family. Obviously, the goal is to let your daughter know that she can approach you

anytime she wants to talk—about anything—but having meals together helps guarantee that communication time.

7. *It leads to better grades and behavior in school.* Families who eat meals together often see higher academic achievements in their children. Showing an active interest in your daughter's life will create a sense of responsibility that carries into her schoolwork and into her life choices as well.

Men should never eat before their families. Before you reach for any food on your dinner table, make sure your family has filled their plates with all the food they want. Even if there is an abundance of food on the table, your family comes first. Start practicing this with your family. If you want to see your daughter grow to be healthy and happy, start putting her first in every part of your life; and there is no better place to start than the dinner table.

After everyone has food on their plates, say a prayer before anyone starts eating. Then you can dig in! Find a topic of discussion for your mealtime. Start off by asking what happened during your daughter's day. Ask your wife how her day was and what she did. Create conversation. Once someone starts talking about her day, everyone should pay attention and be engaged in the conversation.

Nothing is manlier than spending time with your family and teaching them the importance of sharing meals together.

TAKE ACTION

1. Eat meals together with your family.
2. Let your family fill their plates first.

3. Pray before eating.
4. Don't bring phones to the table.
5. Turn the TV off at mealtimes.
6. Create conversation starters.
7. Take time to be present to your family.

CHALLENGE YOURSELF

Your challenge is to make dinner for your family. It does not matter if you have never cooked before or if your wife usually does the cooking. Make dinner for them anyway! Grill something if you have to; just don't make excuses for avoiding this challenge. Start your meal with a prayer. Start a conversation with your family. Listen to what they have to say and then tell them about your day. Share this challenge with them and tell them you are trying to become a more manly man for your family. It might sound silly, but do it anyway and show your family you are proud of trying to improve yourself for their benefit—and yours too!

Manly men take action—do this challenge now!

CHAPTER 8

EXPECT NO TROPHIES

I have heard fathers say that being a father is a thankless job. I completely disagree with this statement. You are not going to win a trophy, get your name in the paper, or win an award for being a father. You are not going to get paid more money, have thousands of people lining up to get your autograph, or become famous by being a father. If that is the sort of reward you are expecting, you are looking in the wrong place. The greatest reward of fatherhood is to raise well-balanced children who are confident, are focused on God, have high moral standards, and love you with all their heart.

There will be times when your daughter will not understand the lessons you are teaching her until much later in life. Teach her anyway. Don't stop doing your job as a father, even if no one points out that you are doing it well.

MY DAUGHTERS' INSIGHT

The other night, I asked my daughters what they considered was the most important thing they had learned from my wife and me — something they would teach their own kids someday.

My girls never disappoint, and as usual, I got some very funny answers.

First, let me set the scene up for you. My youngest daughter was the only one in the room with my wife and me when I asked this question. She instantly responded with, "I feel that love for God was the most important thing you taught me when I was younger, and I will definitely pass that on to my own kids someday."

Then my oldest daughter came into the room, and I asked her the same question. She started off by saying, "How to speak your mind, how to stand up for what you believe in, how to be a good leader, how to fight, how to resolve conflict," and other things like that.

My youngest daughter stared at her sister with open mouth and wondered why she did not mention God. I told her not to say anything, and my oldest daughter said, "What? What am I missing here? Did I miss something?" My youngest daughter could not contain herself any longer and blurted out, "What about God?" My oldest daughter said, "Well, of course God; that goes without saying."

My middle daughter came into the room to see what we were laughing about, and I asked her the same question. Instantly she answered, "I would teach my kids to communicate better than you and Mom do!" I started laughing and said, "What do you mean? Don't you think your mother and I communicate well?" She said, "No, you guys can never decide where you want to go out for dinner!"

We all started laughing, and I said, "So that's all you're going to take away from how you were raised?" Sarcastically, she said "Yes!" My youngest daughter again yelled, "What about God?" My middle daughter added, "Well, of course God," and then started naming a few other things she learned and wanted to pass on to her kids someday, as did my oldest daughter.

Sometimes the lessons you teach your daughter will not seem like lessons to her, as when my oldest and middle daughters did not start off by naming the lesson I had taught them about God. The lessons I taught them about God seemed like second nature to them and part of who they have become.

It's important for fathers to have a realistic expectation of what it means to raise a daughter. If you are expecting all your lessons to be etched on the walls of your daughter's room with a huge banner that reads, "Things my dad taught me," you are going to be very disappointed. That's not the way fatherhood works.

Don't get me wrong. There are certainly times when you will see the result of all your loving care. Actually, you will see it all the time if you pay attention.

It all depends on how needy you are! If you are the type of person who constantly needs to be told he has done a good job, you might be a little frustrated with parenting. If you understand, however, that you are planting seeds and your wisdom will take years and years of growing for your daughter to understand, you will find being a father very fulfilling.

I am not the type of person who needs to be told, "Great job!" I have always felt that doing a job and taking care of my responsibilities was reward enough. When I played baseball in my younger years and got a base hit, I never understood why the coach would say, "Good job!" It was not a good job; it was *the* job. It was the reason I was standing in the batter's box — to get a hit. So when I did what I was expected to do, why should someone have to tell me I did a good job in order for me to appreciate what I did?

The greatest reward a father can have is given to him from God in the form of an opportunity to raise a family. My family has taught me the importance of self-sacrifice, how to put others first, how to love, and much more. I know I have made tons of mistakes, overreacted when I should have been more patient, used bad language at times, and not listened as much as I should have. But I have tried my very best to learn from my mistakes. That's all you can really do as a father.

The one thing I can say without a doubt that I have done for my daughters is to raise them with all the love I have. Every decision, every mistake, every success, was reached by trying my best and keeping my daughters' best interests in mind. I have also always done all I could to make sure they understand my love clearly.

If you do the same, your decisions will not be criticized as much. Not that it matters if anyone criticizes your fathering techniques—after all, you are the man of the house, and as long as you are leading your family toward God and keeping their best interests in mind, you can do no harm.

Manly fathers should never expect anything other than respect from their daughters. In fact, you should demand respect from your daughter. She does not have to agree with your decisions, but she does have to respect them.

Sometimes fathers try to instill fear in their children to make it appear as though they are respected. I feel that is a huge mistake. There will always be a healthy dose of fear mixed in with respect in a good father-daughter relationship. That's the way God's relationship is with us.

When we refrain from sin, it is mostly out of respect mixed with fear of the consequences. For this reason, fathers need to demand respect and set consequences for their daughters.

Causing your daughter to fear you completely is a big mistake. She needs to look up to you as her hero and her protector. She needs to expect all other men in the world to be like you and treat her as you do. And she should never accept anything less. If you are waiting for her to thank you for all the hard work you did as a father, it will be a long wait. When was the last time you thanked your father for the way he raised you? Did you ever specifically thank your father for anything he taught you? If you haven't, there is no time like the present.

A SURPRISING LESSON

My mother told a story about her father when she was growing up. Her father was not a very pleasant man. He was the grandfather I never liked because he always had a miserable outlook on just about everything. I never heard him say he loved me or my mother, and he always seemed upset about something. He had a hard life and a lot of responsibility with four kids to take care of and hardly any money. I am not making excuses for him; he was who he was, and he chose to be that way.

But my mother saw another side of him that none of her brothers or sisters saw. She tells the story of going to a sleepover at a friend's house when she was a teenager and being embarrassed about her pajamas because they were old and torn and the other girls at the sleepover would all have nice pajamas.

Everyone was changing and getting ready for bed when they heard the doorbell ring. A short time later, the parents of the girl who was having the sleepover handed my mom a brown paper bag. They said that her father had brought her pajamas because he noticed she had left hers at home.

She already had her pajamas with her, so what was he dropping off? She took the package and went into the bathroom to change for bed. Opening the bag, she realized that her father had bought her new pajamas and brought them to the sleepover so she would not be embarrassed about her old, torn ones.

My mom's family was dirt poor. But somehow her father was able to buy these pajamas for her. My mom said it was one of the times in her life when she realized what her father sacrificed for her and how he really cared about her feelings.

He left the house without seeing her receive the gift he brought her. He did not need to hear her say thank you. He wanted only to help make his daughter feel happy. What a lesson for a father to learn! No trophies, no awards, only the satisfaction that his daughter was happy.

This story is not about buying a gift for someone. It is about a father seeing a way to make his daughter happy without expecting any sort of thanks in return.

Having heard this story from my mother, I was surprised that her father would have had enough compassion to do something like this, considering the kind of man I thought he was. She said she knew he loved her, even if he hardly ever spoke those words. She also said she saw his love for her family in different ways.

I wish I could say that, as I got older, I learned to like this man more, but I can only say that I love him as Christ asks us to love one another. I just never understood, and probably never will understand, why a father cannot speak the words "I love you" on a daily basis. That needs to be said to your family all the time.

I do, however, understand and have respect for the things my grandfather did to provide for his family. I respect that he sacrificed for his family. He did so without pointing out that he was sacrificing anything for them.

A father cannot selflessly sacrifice for his family if he holds it over their heads all the time and reminds them daily how much he has given up. That is the wrong way to lead your household. Imagine if your wife told you every day that she gave up other guys for you, and that she could be with them instead of sacrificing her life for you. How would that make you feel?

Praising your family without their having to ask for it is very important. Since you are leading by example, once you start praising your family, they will follow your lead and start praising you. Only, don't praise them in order to get praise. Do it because you want to praise them.

What would you do if you owned a business and your employees told you how they could be working at a thousand other places, but instead they choose to sacrifice their life to work for you? If an employee of mine ever came to me with that attitude, I would fix the problem instantly by letting him know he no longer had to sacrifice his life at my business because he no longer worked for me!

The same goes with fatherhood. If you are sacrificing something for your daughter, there is no need to act like a martyr. Sacrifice for the love of helping your daughter, in the same way Jesus sacrificed Himself for us. He did not use His sacrifice as an ultimatum or as a way of controlling us. He sacrificed Himself out of love for us. He sets the perfect example of how a real father, a manly man, should be.

TAKE ACTION

1. Sacrifice unconditionally for your family.
2. Don't expect anything in return.
3. Do not mistake fear for respect.
4. Remember that words alone do not mean as much as actions.

5. Do not have a victim mentality and feel sorry for yourself because you think you are unappreciated.
6. Every day, tell your family you love them.
7. Don't be afraid to show your emotions to your family.
8. Praise your daughter and your wife without their having to ask for it.

CHALLENGE YOURSELF

Your challenge is to pay attention to the way your daughter appreciates the things you do for her. Do not expect a verbal thank-you for every little thing you do. The rewards are visible if you are paying attention. Once you find out how you are being appreciated, thank your daughter for the ways she shows appreciation. For example, if you see her setting the table for your wife, tell her you appreciate her efforts. If you notice that she's doing well in school, let her know you are proud of her. Once your daughter sees you are noticing her efforts without asking for your praise, she will begin noticing the things you do for her. If you want praise, you must also be prepared to give it. Just don't expect it.

Manly men take action—do this challenge now!

CHAPTER 9

BEWARE OF SOCIAL MEDIA

I always think of a trained dog when I see a parent jump to get his phone when it makes a sound. He stops whatever he's doing to make sure he gives his full attention to the person who sent him a message, when the people who really need his attention—his family—are sitting right in front of him.

It's getting worse too! The world is now becoming more "connected" electronically than ever before. In the next ten years, we are going to see "smart" devices in almost all homes as a way to communicate with one another more easily.

I have heard it said that social media is to blame for the distraction of our youth. I disagree. As fathers, we need to be in charge of the amount of time our children spend on social media. In turn, our children need to be responsible enough to put their phones down without being told to do so. It is not the fault of social media that youth are distracted, just as the Fall of man is not the fault of the attractive fruit on the tree in the Garden of Eden.

Social media, when used responsibly, can be a good avenue for business. It can also help families who live far away from one another to connect and communicate. The problem arises when we forget to use social media responsibly. When we forget we are consumers who have been consuming way too much of something, we allow ourselves to be consumed.

For the sake of argument, let's compare social media to food. Imagine that every time you go on social media, you take a bite of food. By the end of the day, how much food would you have consumed? Would it be healthful for you, or would you be obese in a week? Are you consuming your social media responsibly?

When you are with your family, be present. Put down the phone and give your daughter the attention she desperately needs and deserves. Spending time on the phone when you should be spending time with your daughter sends the message that she is less important than social media. This is a dangerous message to convey.

One thing that really irritates me is to see a man who is with his family but is on his phone instead of paying attention to them. I have seen entire families out to dinner together, and instead of talking to one another, all of them are on a phone, or on a tablet, or on some other device that robs them of time together.

Social media is a big problem with girls today. The amount of time many girls spend trying to take the perfect photo of themselves from different angles and posting it online, only to remove it minutes later because they are not getting enough likes, is staggering. The pressure many young girls put on themselves to reach this false image of online perfection and seek the approval of others is damaging to their self-confidence.

Years ago, this issue did not exist. Constantly being criticized by peer groups was not something girls in past generations had to deal with. They were able to disconnect and spend much-needed time away from overly critical peers. Nowadays, girls are in never-ending contact with everyone.

Overuse of social media platforms ends up chipping away at the confidence and moral fiber fathers strive to build in their daughters. All the hard work you have done can be wiped away quicker than you may believe. Social media anxiety is brought on by girls feeling trapped by the "need" they seem to have for the approval of their peers.

The lines of moral and modest behavior can easily be blurred within the realm of social media. Girls are constantly seeking the approval of their peers for photos they post online, and they seem to take more and more risqué photos of themselves to get more likes. Girls endanger themselves by attempting to complete online challenges they see other people doing, such as the "thigh-gap challenge" in which girls are expected to have a gap of a certain width between their thighs in a photo. Some girls develop eating disorders trying to achieve these ridiculous goals. Although these fads come and go, girls seem to get caught up in being able to do what they see others do and to look the way they see others look online.

This creates an environment that is unhealthy and damaging both physically and mentally, not to mention spiritually, for these young girls. Instead of keeping their focus on God and having self-confidence, they slowly start to worry about others' impressions of who they are and to try constantly to please other people.

The overexposure to social media starts at a young age for girls. Whether they are posting photos publicly, or sending private messages, they seem to be constantly online in one way or another. Peer pressure is a major cause of this. Since everyone else is online, girls feel the need to communicate with their friends there as well. You are responsible for teaching your daughter about the dangers of social media and helping her to avoid them.

Many times, the younger generation complains that parents just don't understand. This may be true in the case of social media and the effects it seems to be having on young girls. We may, in fact, not understand the potential depth of damage. That's the scary part. Since online communication via social media is so new, it is hard to say what long-term effects it will have on girls. What we do know is how they are being affected presently, and the results are very worrisome. If the current effects of social media on girls are any indication of how girls will be affected in the future, we need to do a better job of teaching our daughters about these dangers at a young age.

WAS I ADDICTED?

Being addicted to social media is not something that many young girls will admit to; in fact, it is not something that many adults will admit to. Not admitting to this type of addiction is just like not admitting to any other addiction. It's hard for someone with any addiction to be aware of his addiction in the first place.

I did not feel as if I was addicted to social media, since I went online only from time to time and did not really stay on very long. That was until I started paying attention to how much time I was spending on social media. I wanted to see whether I was losing track of time while on social media without being aware of it. When I calculated the amount of real time I spent online, it was eye-opening to say the least.

At home, I would go on social media many times a day. At work, I would be on social media during every break and during most of my lunch hour. Surprisingly, I even checked my social media accounts whenever I got to a red light in traffic. I did not do this while driving, but whenever I stopped, I was online, seeing what people were saying about whatever topic they felt was important enough to share with the world.

BEWARE OF SOCIAL MEDIA

After one day, I added up the amount of time I spent on social media, and, to my surprise, it totaled more than two and a half hours. I thought this had to be an error on my part, so I added the numbers again. Nope, I was right the first time. Incredible! I had no idea I was online this much and doing absolutely nothing that was anywhere near productive for more than two and a half hours a day. I am always telling my daughters that they need to be aware of what they do with their time, and here I was wasting two and a half hours a day.

I did some quick figuring and realized a horrible truth: at this rate, in ten days, I would have wasted an entire day. So, since I began using social media ten years ago, I had wasted one-tenth of my time—one full year of my life! Do the math—it's scary!

Immediately I realized that social media addiction was more dangerous than a lot of addictions because it goes unnoticed for so long and seems very natural while it is happening. This realization demanded an instant change in my life. After all, time is the most valuable resource we have, and we cannot afford to waste any of it. I took out my phone and deleted all my personal social media accounts.

I also let my daughters know what I found out about the time I was wasting and showed them that I had deleted all my social media accounts. My middle daughter pulled out her phone and instantly got rid of two of the four social media platforms she was using. She said she didn't need them and felt they were wasting her time as well.

On my first day without social media, I honestly felt a little awkward. When I would normally be on social media, I had nothing to do. At home in the morning, I looked at a few old photo albums or found a book to read. During my lunch hour, I started contacting business clients whom I had not talked to in a while to see if they wanted to do more business. The most shocking realization came to me when I got to a red light while I was driving home. I reached for my phone, picked it up, and looked at it. This was done completely out of habit and muscle memory, mindlessly. I did not realize how much of a slave I had become to my social media accounts.

I resolved to do something productive with my newfound time. Actually, the time had always been there; I just chose not to waste it any longer. A colleague and I had been writing a book, and in more than a year of working on it, I was never able to find the time or concentrate on it enough to finish. Within three weeks of breaking away from social media, however, I had not only finished writing the book but had also self-published it, designed a cover, and had the first run printed.[1]

It's amazing what you can get done when you weed out the distractions in your life.

IS YOUR DAUGHTER ADDICTED?

Just because your daughter uses social media does not mean she is addicted. It is important to watch for warning signs of addiction, but just because she likes to see what her friends are up to from time to time does not indicate a problem.

The amount of time your daughter spends on her phone, combined with her perceived "need" to use social media, can be a good indicator of whether there is cause for concern. Here are a few other warning signs of social media addiction.

[1] See *Teaching Teens to Fail: The 5-Step Field Guide for Parenting Success.*

BEWARE OF SOCIAL MEDIA

1. *Constantly checking notifications, sharing photos, playing games, or posting status updates.* Being constantly distracted from real-life issues and *obsessing* over social media updates is one warning sign. Simply being distracted from time to time is not unusual with girls, but the extent of these distractions can tell a lot about how serious this addiction may be. Watch for complete distraction and lack of personal awareness.

2. *Complete disconnect from real-life issues and interactions.* The lack of social skills and real-life communication skills is apparent in many young girls today. Even though it is necessary, face-to-face interaction is becoming less and less important to them. Overusing social media causes a certain disconnect from real-life experiences.

3. *Obsession with online videos or memes, and constantly talking in "meme talk."* If your daughter constantly refers to memes she saw online and expects everyone to understand what she's talking about, as if they had the same experience she did, she may be spending too much time online. Being unaware that anyone would be disconnected from social media and online interaction and expecting everyone to have seen the same things she has in her own online "world" may be cause for concern.

4. *Withdrawing from sports, clubs, or offline activities.* If your daughter has suddenly stopped playing a sport or has quit an afterschool club or activity, without speaking to you about it beforehand, so she can spend more time online with her friends, there may be cause for concern.

5. *Obsession with posting photos and status updates.* Simply taking a photo or updating a status from time to time is not a problem. If, however, you notice your daughter taking hundreds of photos of herself to post the perfect one online, only to remove it because she is not getting enough likes, you may need to bring this to her attention.

Just remember: there has to be a good balance with social media usage. It's no different from anything else your daughter is interested in. If she is overexposed and obsessed with anything in her life, intervention is called for.

Being a manly father means having the courage to discuss these things with your daughter without fearing that you are being overbearing. If what you are doing is out of love for your daughter, she will understand the restrictions and limitations you place on her use of social media.

SOLUTIONS

This social media epidemic may seem at first to be incurable. The way girls connect with their friends today is mostly online. Does this mean that they should not be allowed to connect in this manner at all? Not necessarily. There are ways to educate your daughter and make her aware of the amount of time she spends on social media, as well as the possible dangers of addiction.

Although the ultimate decision will be up to your daughter, as you cannot be with her every minute of her life, there are some ways to help reduce her exposure to social media and the amount of time she spends on it.

BEWARE OF SOCIAL MEDIA

1. *Limit the number of social media networks your daughter is on.* Instead of having five social media accounts, limit her to one or two. This will not completely stop the overuse of social media, but it will reduce it greatly.
2. *Turn off notifications.* Not having your daughter's phone buzz or make a sound every time one of her friends sends out new information or posts something can help reduce the "trained dog" reaction that so many people seem to have when their phones make a sound.
3. *Find a new hobby.* Readings books is a great hobby. Maybe your daughter hasn't thrown a Frisbee, played a sport, or ridden her bicycle in a long time. Anything that gets the phone out of her hand and helps her concentrate on something different can be beneficial. Maybe she could even write a book!
4. *Set a timer for her.* Give her fifteen minutes at a time, and only three or four times a day, to check her social media accounts. Fifteen minutes, four times a day equals one hour per day. Don't put these fifteen-minute increments right next to each other; spread them throughout the day to ensure healthy time away from social media.
5. *Spend more family time together.* Find things to do together with your daughter and create family time. This not only distracts the family from social media but has the additional benefit of helping you bond with your daughter. For this to work, you both need to stay off your phones while you spend time together.

6. *Consider whether she needs a smartphone.* Most fathers want to be able to give their daughters the best of everything. If all of your daughter's friends have smartphones, then she must need one too, right? Wrong! Just because every other girl in the universe seems to have a smartphone, it does not mean that your daughter needs one. It's easy to confuse "need" and "want." Help your daughter to understand that she *wants* a smartphone but does not *need* one. Getting her a good old-fashioned flip phone or one that does not allow apps and social media at all can be another way to prevent overexposure.

7. *Quit completely.* If nothing else seems to work with your daughter's social media addiction, forbidding its use completely will definitely do the trick. This must be a last-ditch effort because taking her friend connections away completely can be just as damaging as having too much online friend time. Sometimes, however, there is no option other than cutting her off completely for a certain time. Once she has gone through her withdrawal from being removed completely from social media, you can start reintroducing one social media network at a time with the knowledge that there will be set time limits as well as restrictions on which social media platforms you are comfortable with her using.

Some of these suggestions may seem a bit much for you. It may be uncomfortable to suggest something for your daughter that you are not doing yourself. Guess what? That means it's time to lead by example and stop using your phone so much. What sort of example do you want to give your daughter to follow?

BEWARE OF SOCIAL MEDIA

Words are weak. If you want to see a change in your daughter's online habits, you must change yours. It is not easy to make a change, especially one that you might think is not necessary.

TAKE ACTION

1. Educate your daughter about social media addiction.
2. Get involved with your daughter's online interactions and postings.
3. Watch for signs that your daughter is becoming obsessed with the desire to get others' approval of her appearance.
4. Know which social media platforms your daughter is on and how often she posts on these sites.
5. Encourage your daughter to become engaged in offline activities, such as sports, clubs, and so forth.
6. Limit the amount of time your daughter spends online.
7. Challenge your daughter to restrict herself from being online as much as she currently is.
8. Lead by example—get off the phone and into your daughter's life!

CHALLENGE YOURSELF

Your challenge is to cut your social media time in half. The ultimate goal is not to use any at all, other than occasionally for business or for connecting with out-of-town family. Stop posting senseless things and status updates. Get rid of the things that are distracting you from being manly. A real man understands that he is in control of his life. He is not a slave to anything or anyone. A real man challenges his daughter to hold herself to a higher standard. Once you have completed your challenge of cutting your social media time in half, challenge your daughter to cut her social media time in half as well. Good luck, and remember to be manly!

Manly men take action—do this challenge now!

CHAPTER 10

TEST YOUR KNOWLEDGE

Are you a manly man? Be honest with your answers below and find out the truth!

- Does your family go to church together regularly?
- Have you ever brought your daughter flowers?
- When was the last time you brought your wife flowers?
- What is your daughter's favorite sport?
- How tall is your daughter?
- Who is your daughter's best friend?
- If your daughter could pick any place to go on vacation, where would it be?
- When is your daughter's birthday?
- What is your daughter's favorite flavor of ice cream?
- What is your daughter's favorite restaurant?
- What is your daughter's shoe size?
- Who is your daughter's favorite musician or band?
- Does your daughter have a crush on a boy? If so, what is his name?
- How old is your daughter?
- Does your daughter ask for your advice?
- What makes your daughter angry?
- What is your daughter's favorite place to go?

- What is your daughter's biggest fear? Does she know your biggest fear?
- What is your daughter's best subject at school? What is her worst subject at school?
- Who is your daughter's favorite teacher? Who is her least favorite teacher?
- What is your daughter's favorite family memory?
- What does your daughter think your best quality is? What does she think your worst quality is?
- What is your daughter's proudest moment?
- What career does your daughter want to have when she grows up?
- Is your daughter happy?
- Have you told your daughter you are proud of her? If so, did you tell her exactly why?
- Do you tell your daughter each day that you love her?
- What is your daughter's biggest regret?
- Does your daughter have a diary?
- If your daughter could choose only one food to eat forever, what would it be?
- What is your daughter's favorite time of day?

How did you score on the test? Do you know your daughter's likes and dislikes, or do you need to find the answers to these questions? Remember, the point of finding out these answers is not to check off a box and move on to the next question; the enjoyment comes from learning about your daughter. Take time to get to know her.

Once you feel you have a great understanding of who your daughter is, ask her the same questions to see how well she knows you. Obviously, some will not apply to you, but ask her the ones that do apply. Don't be afraid to stop in the middle of the test to have a discussion. Remember, building a relationship with your daughter is not a sprint; it's a marathon. Take whatever time is necessary to get to know your daughter better.

In fact, take a second right now to do something manly. Call your daughter into the room right now and tell her you love her. If she is not at home, call her on the phone and tell her you love her. If she is in school right now, text her and tell her you love her. Whatever you are doing right this second, stop and let her know you love her.

Great job! Now—another manly moment! Do the same with your wife. Call her and tell her you love her; or if she is there with you, hug her and tell her you appreciate her and love her. It really does not matter if you had an argument this morning or not; tell her you love her anyway.

I am not very fond of texting. I have never liked it. My hands and fingers are way too large to hit the right letters, and I feel that texting is impersonal at times. Recently, however, I have been making a point of texting my daughters daily and saying, "I just wanted to let you know I am very proud of you, and I love you very much," or something to that effect.

The first time I sent this text to my daughters, they all texted back a few minutes later with hilarious responses. My oldest daughter said, "What's wrong? I love you too, but what's wrong?" My middle daughter said, "Why are you texting me this? Are you okay?" When I responded that I was fine and just wanted to say hi, she said, "You are so weird ... lol ... but I love you too." My youngest daughter responded with, "What's happening? I love you too, but is everything all right?" It took about a week or so of texting them to tell them I love them for my daughters to realize nothing was wrong.

We were all sitting and eating dinner one night when the topic came up about my texting them daily. They were laughing about something I did or said at dinner, and my youngest daughter mentioned that when I send her a text, it makes her think something is wrong. My middle daughter said, "I like it. You can keep texting me, Dad; I don't mind." My oldest daughter said she just worried because she knows I do not like to text and thought something was wrong.

I told them I was just letting them know I was thinking about them, and since I knew they primarily texted instead of talking on the phone, I thought I would try texting instead of calling.

In youth ministry, this is called "meeting them where they are." That means you need to reach out to youth to communicate with them in the way they spend time communicating. It also means they have a lot to learn about how to think and act as an adult, and you need to be there to guide them along the right path. Reach out to your daughter, but don't expect her to be where you are mentally, emotionally, or spiritually. It will happen in time, so be patient. And, of course, lead by example!

CHALLENGE YOURSELF

Your challenge is to get a perfect score on these questions, no matter how long it takes. Get to know who your daughter is. Let her know you are interested in her life. Don't be afraid to let her know you want to get to know her better. She needs you in her life. Start being manly right now, and get to work!

Manly men take action—do this challenge now!

CHAPTER 11

Cultivate Manly Qualities

The word "man" is used very loosely in our vocabulary. Someone can be considered a man because he is the strongest, drinks the most beer, sleeps with the most women, has the broadest shoulders, is tallest in a crowd, has the deepest voice or the fastest car, makes the most money, and so forth. But rarely is the word used correctly.

I have heard "men" I know say they are tired of being married to their wives because they are not being satisfied at home as they "deserve" to be. I have seen "men" leave their families to raise themselves because these men don't want to face their own responsibilities. I have also seen countless women throw themselves at "men" so they can feel a sense of belonging and acceptance, even when that means losing sight of who they really are.

There are men who never show up for their daughters' dance recitals because the recitals are "too boring" or because they interfere with their golf plans for the day. There are men who have never seen their daughters practice or play a sport, taken their daughters to father-daughter dances, or been a field trip chaperone. Is this manly? No.

Men struggle with setting a good example for their families because they lead a double life. Some men have a "do as I say, not as I do" attitude. They tell their daughters that it is wrong to look at pornography, but they are doing just that when no one is looking. They tell their daughters that it is wrong to get drunk, but they get drunk every weekend. They tell their daughters that smoking and using drugs is wrong, but when no one is around, they are doing what they preach against publicly.

Manly men tell the truth at all times. They are not ashamed of their actions in private. Would you honestly be proud of showing your daughter everything you do in private when you think no one is watching? What about your wife? Would she be proud of your behaviors? If you don't think God already sees everything you are doing, you have a huge awakening coming your way eventually. Manly men do what is right, even when no one is watching.

Years ago, I coached a basketball team for my daughter that went undefeated for several seasons in a row. When other coaches would ask my secret to winning all these games and championships, I would tell them that when you have champions playing for your team, it's easy to win all the time. Usually, these coaches would not push their questioning any further, but I have had a few coaches and parents ask what I did to create champions.

I let them know, first and foremost, that we always started practice and games with a prayer. At practice, when the girls were tired or wanted to give up, I told them somthing that seemed to resonate with them. I said, "Champions are made when no one is watching. They are made when everyone else has left the gym; long after the lights have gone down and long after all the press has left the building. It's what you do when no one is watching that really matters. Do the right thing!"

Champions live in the truth. When no one is watching a practice, when autographs are not being signed, and when you are doing things that make a real difference for yourself, that's when the truth of your situation sinks in. Just because you can talk a good game, that doesn't mean you can play one too. Take a minute and relate this to how you are performing as a father. Do you talk a good game in public but act very differently when no one is watching? Do you have certain expectations for your daughter and your wife that you are not living up to? Only you can make the changes needed in your life to make a real difference for them. It's time to start speaking the truth at all times, no matter what.

SEVEN MANLY QUALITIES

1. *A focus on God.* Do you keep God first? Do you teach your daughter to do the same?
2. *Loyalty.* Do you cheat on your wife, or are you true to your family commitments?
3. *Honesty.* Do you lie? This includes lying to yourself.
4. *Kindness.* Are you kind, or are you nice? Being kind means being strong enough to tell the truth at all times out of love. Being nice means saying and doing things out of fear of hurting feelings. Niceness lacks love.
5. *Generosity.* Do you give of yourself to your family, or are you a taker?
6. *Bravery.* Are you brave enough to teach your daughter to speak her mind, or do you teach her to go with the flow?

7. *Cleanness.* Are you clean in body, mind, and spirit? Or are you leading a dirty double life behind closed doors?

If you have not considered these points before, I challenge you as a manly father to do so right now.

Society has forgotten what a real man is. Hopefully by reading this book, you have gained a better understanding of the qualities a manly father needs to exhibit—not only for himself, but for his daughter as well.

Now is the time for self-reflection and being honest. Do you need to work on these traits? Would you be willing to ask your family how they think you are doing as a dad? Would you be willing to humble yourself enough to listen without getting angry, or debating how they view your successes and failures as a father?

How many people in your life offer you complete honesty whether you ask for it or not? How many people are you completely honest with? If your daughter is not one of these people, you may be trying to hide the real you from everyone, including yourself. It is never too late to make changes in your life and in the life of your daughter by being the type of man she can be proud of.

CHALLENGE YOURSELF

Your challenge from now on is to tell the truth at all times—no matter what. Start by being honest with yourself and be proud of who you are. If you are honest with yourself and proud of the type of man you are, your daughter will be proud of you as well. Treat your wife with respect and show your daughter what it looks like to tell the truth all the time. Show her what it looks like to be truly manly!

Manly men take action—do this challenge now!

Thank you for taking the time to read *The Manly Art of Raising a Daughter*. Tell a friend about this book and share with him a challenge or two from a previous chapter. If someone gave you this book as a gift, thank that person for helping you become a better man, a manly man.

Remember that iron sharpens iron, and, as men, we need to sharpen one another. Holding one another to a challenge of complete honesty at all times is the only way men can be truly manly.

ABOUT THE AUTHOR

Alan Migliorato has been married to the same beautiful woman since 1993 and has three gorgeous daughters. He has owned a sign and advertising company based in the Orlando, Florida, area for the past twenty years. He has a certification in youth ministry from the University of Dayton and is the founder of Adventure Catholic Leadership Formation Training. Alan achieved the rank of Eagle Scout and is a veteran of the U.S. Army. He offers motivational speaking engagements, as well as parent-teen retreat weekends and team-building camps. His passions are his family and leading others to Jesus.

Sophia Institute

Sophia Institute is a nonprofit institution that seeks to nurture the spiritual, moral, and cultural life of souls and to spread the Gospel of Christ in conformity with the authentic teachings of the Roman Catholic Church.

Sophia Institute Press fulfills this mission by offering translations, reprints, and new publications that afford readers a rich source of the enduring wisdom of mankind.

Sophia Institute also operates two popular online Catholic resources: CrisisMagazine.com and CatholicExchange.com.

Crisis Magazine provides insightful cultural analysis that arms readers with the arguments necessary for navigating the ideological and theological minefields of the day. *Catholic Exchange* provides world news from a Catholic perspective as well as daily devotionals and articles that will help you to grow in holiness and live a life consistent with the teachings of the Church.

In 2013, Sophia Institute launched Sophia Institute for Teachers to renew and rebuild Catholic culture through service to Catholic education. With the goal of nurturing the spiritual, moral, and cultural life of souls, and an abiding respect for the role and work of teachers, we strive to provide materials and programs that are at once enlightening to the mind and ennobling to the heart; faithful and complete, as well as useful and practical.

Sophia Institute gratefully recognizes the Solidarity Association for preserving and encouraging the growth of our apostolate over the course of many years. Without their generous and timely support, this book would not be in your hands.

www.SophiaInstitute.com
www.CatholicExchange.com
www.CrisisMagazine.com
www.SophiaInstituteforTeachers.org

Sophia Institute Press® is a registered trademark of Sophia Institute.
Sophia Institute is a tax-exempt institution as defined by the
Internal Revenue Code, Section 501(c)(3). Tax I.D. 22-2548708.